Harry Ford

A history of the Harriet Hollond memorial Presbyterian church of

Philadelphia

Harry Ford

A history of the Harriet Hollond memorial Presbyterian church of Philadelphia

ISBN/EAN: 9783337126124

Printed in Europe, USA, Canada, Australia, Japan

Cover: Foto ©Andreas Hilbeck / pixelio.de

More available books at **www.hansebooks.com**

A HISTORY

OF THE

HARRIET HOLLOND

MEMORIAL

PRESBYTERIAN CHURCH

OF

PHILADELPHIA, PA.

BY

HARRY PRINGLE FORD

PHILADELPHIA
CASTLE & HEILMAN
PRINTERS
27 NORTH SECOND ST.
1899

BLESSED BE THE GOD AND FATHER OF OUR LORD
JESUS CHRIST, WHO HATH BLESSED US WITH ALL
SPIRITUAL BLESSINGS..

—EPHESIANS 1: 3.

TO THE

CHRISTIAN MEN AND WOMEN

WHOSE FAITHFULNESS IN THE PAST

HAS MADE OUR BELOVED CHURCH

WHAT IT NOW IS;

TO

THOSE WHO IN THE PRESENT

ARE STRIVING WITH UNWAVERING DEVOTION

TO INCREASE ITS USEFULNESS;

AND TO

ALL WHO IN THE FUTURE

SHALL AID IN ITS DIVINE MISSION

OF SAVING SOULS,

THIS VOLUME

IS AFFECTIONATELY DEDICATED.

The Golden Age lies *onward*, not *behind*.
The pathway through the Past has led us *up*.
The pathway through the Future will lead *on*
And *higher*. * * *
If we but fight the wrong, and keep the faith,
And battle for the Future, all mankind
Will bless us in the days that are to come.

—JAMES A. EDGERTON.

CONTENTS

NOTE

The story of the inception and development of the Hollond Memorial Church is here told for the simple purpose of perpetuating the record of a noble work for the Master. The hope is expressed that it will incite to higher spiritual usefulness all who read its pages.

A great field is about us; a great duty calls us. *Let us go onward!*

H. P. F.

· Philadelphia, Pa.,

December 1899.

THE MOYAMENSING MISSION

The Moyamensing Mission School, of which the Hollond Memorial Church is the outgrowth, was organized by members of the old Tenth Presbyterian Church, and first met in a small hall on Christian street, near Tenth. The Rev. A. P. Happer, D. D., who was afterwards known throughout the entire Presbyterian Church by his nearly fifty years of missionary service in China and who died in Wooster, Ohio, October 27, 1894, at the age of 76, was one of the first superintendents. In a letter dated October 17, 1893, Dr. Happer wrote: "In November, 1842, at the request of the teachers, I commenced the duties of superintendent. The hall in which we met was used on week-days for all kinds of secular purposes, often till late on Saturday nights. Some of the teachers had to go on Sunday before school-time to clean it up, and get it ready for the scholars; and then had to go through the streets to gather in the children."

Dr. Happer mentioned William H. Mitchell John McArthur and family, Daniel Mallery,

"the indefatigable visitor and worker," and
Thomas Jones, as being his early associates in
the work. John Culbert was one of the first
and most active workers, and his daughter
Elizabeth, now Mrs. Williams, attended the
first session as a scholar. Paul T. Jones was
also an able helper.

The school continued to meet in the hall,
which was at that time on the southern out-
skirts of the city, for about three years, and
then was removed to a public room opposite.
Shortly after, it was again removed to the second floor of a fire hose-house, occupied by the
Native American Hose Company, on the south
side of Carpenter street, below Tenth. The
neighborhood was a most unpleasant one, as
men and boys frequently congregated on the
open lots and fought along the streets.

In 1847, Mr. Maurice A. Wurts was elected
to the superintendency, several persons having
filled that position subsequent to the resignation of Dr. Happer. Mr. Wurts conducted
the school with signal ability for eleven years,
and was quite as strong a factor in its success
as Mr. Morris and Mr. Ogden afterwards became. It numbered less than sixty scholars
when he became the leader, and the room in
which it met was not only cheerless, but almost
destitute of furniture—unless plain board
benches could be so called. He succeeded,

however, in securing a large and efficient force of teachers, and soon after a building costing $1,800 was erected on Carpenter street, adjoining the hose-house. It was dedicated in June, 1848. A parish school, numbering at times as many as one hundred scholars, was formed and maintained for several years. Miss Margaret Thompson, (now Mrs. Mason), was the first principal. In 1849, Miss Elizabeth N. Brown became interested in the work and taught a girls' Bible class for some three years. She was then appointed assistant superintendent, and held that position until 1865. By her untiring efforts in visiting the scholars in their homes and the interest she took in the families connected with the school, she did much to promote its general prosperity. Two rooms were added to the rear of the main building in 1854, at a cost of $1,100. At that time the names of 232 scholars were on the roll. The largest attendance during the year was 226, and the average attendance 166. The collections amounted to $80.51. The library numbered 700 volumes.

In May, 1854, Mr. Wurts thus writes: "The school will compare favorably with other Sabbath-schools in regard to punctuality, order and progress. The scholars come not by compulsion, but from love of the school. We have ascertained in several instances in visiting that the greatest punishment their parents can impose, is to refuse them permission to attend. Our semi-monthly examinations show commendable progress in the study of the Catechism.

"Only a few years ago, many who now compose our number, were to be found in the street on the Sabbath, ignorant, ill-clad, and ill-behaved; they are now respectful and obedient, well-clothed and cleanly, and in their appearance and deportment will compare most favorably with those ordinarily seen in a regular church Sunday-school. Above all, they have received, and are receiving, much instruction, and we trust it will yet be seen that the efforts put forth have been the means, under God, of bringing many from nature's darkness to the marvelous light of the Gospel. In a word, we think a great work has been already accomplished, and that much is still being done for the spiritual and temporal good of this entire neighborhood through the instrumentality of the enterprise which the liberality and countenance of the Tenth Church have so long sustained."

At that time the officers of the school were : Maurice A. Wurts, superintendent ; William L. Mactier, vice-superintendent ; William Mason and James McAllister, librarians ; Charles W. Leavitt, secretary. The teachers were

Messrs. H. M. Olmstead, John Mason, Edward Orne, William L. Hildeburn, William L. Mactier, Jared Craig, Robert Nichol, John A. McAllister, John W. Reed, Wilson Dunton, John H. Brown, John Wescott, Mrs. Ellen Reynolds, and Misses Margaret Thompson, Ellen Thompson, Elizabeth N. Brown, Harriette Wurts, Elizabeth Grier, C. D. McLaughlin, Sarah Taylor, E. L. Dickinson, Mary Young, Lydia S. Penrose, Mary Brown, Mary Briscoe, Mary Linnard, Emily Leavitt, Agnes M. Goertner (lost at sea on a French steamer), and Miss McFetrick. Mr. Samuel H. Fulton succeeded Mr. Wurts as superintendent.

From 1855 to 1862, the school attained its greatest early prosperity, numbering at one time nearly six hundred scholars. A spirit of generosity was inculcated and the children were encouraged to aid in the furtherance of outside benevolences. For many years a portion of the collections was devoted to the support of a boy in China, Ah Chung, who received the name of Mitchell Wurts (after two of our superintendents). He was adopted by Dr. Happer, and afterwards became an assistant in the medical work. A case of surgical instruments was presented to him by our school. Dr. Happer's letters relative to him were always listened to with intense interest by the scholars. He was baptized and married in the same year, 1854. His was the first Christian marriage in Canton. He became the father of several children, one of whom was educated in America by the Chinese government.

On the 27th of October, 1856, Dr. Boardman, pastor of the Tenth Church, wrote the following letter to the Rev. Willard M. Rice, D. D., who had been for sixteen years proprietor and principal of a classical school at the south-east corner of Ninth and Arch streets, and who had also been actively engaged in church and Sunday-school work:

" MY DEAR SIR:

"The teachers of our mission school on Carpenter street, below 10th, wish to secure the services of a minister or licentiate to preach there and do the work of an evangelist. I do not know whether it would suit you to labor there, or whether your gifts and style of preaching would suit the place. But with an excellent building erected for the purpose (the property of my church), a very flourishing school, with an efficient corps of teachers, and a prosperous neighborhood, the field is really one of much promise.

"It has occurred to me that it might be agreeable to you to preach there on some Sabbath evening; and, if so, I beg to ask whether you could go on next Sabbath week, the 9th proximo? As they have no preaching there ordinarily, the arrangement should be made the Sabbath before."

Dr. Rice visited the school on November 2d,

REV. WILLARD M. RICE, D. D.

and, after an interview with the officers and teachers, accepted the invitation to hold service on the 9th. He took for his text John 6: 37. "Him that cometh to me I will in no wise cast out." Many of the teachers, scholars and parents were present, making in all a congregation of one hundred and seventy-five.

On the 17th of November Dr. Boardman thus wrote to Dr. Rice:

"It has given me much pleasure to learn how acceptable your ministrations have been to the people at our Moyamensing mission."

Dr. Rice engaged to labor as an evangelist in the neighborhood, especially among the families connected with the Sabbath-school. Services were held every Sabbath evening, and four afternoons each week were spent in visiting the families whose children were connected with the school. Maurice A. Wurts, the superintendent, was a very earnest, devoted Christian. He was greatly beloved by the teachers and scholars of the mission. He afterwards became an elder in the Woodland Church, and was for many years missionary secretary of the American Sunday-school Union. Miss Brown, who is still living, was also devotedly attached to the work. In 1865 she went to Bethany school where she has since labored with great fidelity and success. A more faithful company of Sabbath-school teachers could not be found. Messrs. Wurts, Fulton, Hoyt, McMillan, Mason, Craig, Leavitt, Balbirnie, and the Misses Penrose, Grier, Mary and Fanny Brown, McArthur, Hazzard, and Mrs. Fulton, assisted in carrying on the work of visitation. The enthusiastic interest of Mr. Charles Balbirnie was specially helpful at this time.

During Dr. Rice's seven years' connection with the work a large Bible class was taught at different times by Mr. McMillan, Peter Walker, Dr. J. G. Kerr, now, and for more than forty years, a medical missionary in China, and Mr. F. A. Packard, the corresponding secretary of the American Sunday-school Union. Every Saturday afternoon during the winter season a sewing school was conducted by the lady teachers, and much help was thus rendered in supplying clothes to the needy. The spirit of Christ was in all the work.

During the winter of 1856-7, there were much suffering and want among the poor families connected with the mission, which the teachers did much to relieve. Dr. Rice attended every session of the school—often teaching when teachers were absent. The teachers, however, were remarkably regular and prompt in their attendance. Nearly all of them were members of the Tenth Church and lived at a considerable distance from the

school. Some, however, were members of
other churches, among them being Miss Agnes
Ashman, (who died Feb. 12th, 1897). She
was a sister of Judge Ashman, and a member
of a Baptist church. She gave devoted service to the school in the Infant Department.

The pastor and session of the Tenth Church
were uniformly friendly, and were deeply interested in the welfare of the mission. Every
year a Christmas festival was held, which was
attended in crowds by the children and by the
friends and supporters of the school in the
Tenth Church. It was a red-letter day with
all; as were also the anniversary days, which
were celebrated every spring in the Tenth
Church.

Very frequently during the first two winters
the water in the gas-meter would be found
frozen when the room was to be lighted.
Very often Dr. Rice would have to borrow a
kettle of hot water from a neighboring house
to thaw the ice. He was then living some
three miles from the field. One snowy winter
night he and his son (who afterwards became
a surgeon in the U. S. Navy, and died at sea
on the man-of-war " Ossipee," July 13th,
1868), walked (there being no cars) down to
the mission, thawed out the meter, and held
service. The thermometer was down almost
to zero. Only five other persons were present.

A PERSONAL REMINISCENCE

W. D. Hoyt, M. D., of Rome, Ga , one of the first
elders of the old Moyamensing Church and a teacher
in the school, in a letter written in January, 1899, thus
describes this period:

" I do not remember in what year I first
became connected with Moyamensing Sunday-
school. It was during Mr. Wurts' superintendency, and in response to an appeal made
by Dr. Boardman for teachers, that I offered
myself and was accepted. The school seemed
to be in a flourishing condition, the attendance being quite large. It was then occupy-
ing the building on Carpenter street. I was
given a class of eight or ten boys—pretty
rough little fellows, full of fun and mischief.
There were considerable poverty and want in
the neighborhood, and there were many bar-
rooms. The people generally belonged to the
laboring classes, and were in need of the uplifting power of applied Christianity.

" I have a distinct recollection of the violent
abuse I received from the infidel father of one
of my boys. The boy had been absent from
Sunday-school, and I had called on him in

W. D. HOYT, M. D.

consequence. The father came in whilst I was there, and proceeded to open the vials of his abuse upon me. His wife was much afraid that he would strike me as he threatened to do. I thought it was my duty to take the abuse, but had mentally drawn the line at a blow— and I was pretty well up in boxing. However, he did not strike me.

"I recollect the earnest discussion we had when it was proposed to organize a church. I was solicited to become an elder. I was quite young and hesitated on that account; but it was presented to me so strongly as a matter of duty that I had to consent. The church was accordingly organized in 1858, Dr. W. M. Rice being the pastor and Mr. Samuel H. Fulton and I the two elders. At the time it was proposed to organize a church the neighborhood was thoroughly canvassed, but there was found to be only a very small sprinkling of Protestants. Whether it was from an anti-Protestant feeling or the natural perversity of boys, I know not, but it was not at all unusual to have our evening services disturbed by the throwing of stones at the building. I recollect on one occasion, when the stone-throwing was particularly violent, my making a sally and chasing the fleeing boys across some vacant lots; my capturing a little fellow and threatening to take him into the

church, and finally releasing him at his
frightened pleadings. I think this episode
had a good effect in stopping the stone-throwing. Dr. Rice did not seem much disturbed
by such occurrences, but continued his sermons
uninterruptedly.

"We had preaching morning and evening on
Sunday, Sunday-school in the afternoon, and
prayer-meeting Wednesday evening. There
was a gradual growth and development in the
church. I remained with it until 1861, when
anticipations of the war led me to arrange to
come South to my own people. I have been
in Philadelphia only once since, and regret
very much that I did not re-visit the church on
that occasion. Should I chance to visit it
again, I shall certainly go to the Hollond Memorial Church, and endeavor to absorb some of
the enthusiasm and zeal with which it seems to
be so fully imbued. Let me extend to you my
hearty congratulations for the achievements of
the past, and my best wishes for your continued success in turning many souls to right-
eousness. May the labors of the pastors, superintendents and teachers be crowned with
God's richest blessings!"

It had long been a cherished wish of the teachers that the school should develop into a church. Many of the pupils, and some of the parents, had become hopeful Christians and had united with various churches.

The attendance on the services during the first winter of Dr. Rice's labors (1856), averaged 125; it afterwards became much larger. Morning services were not held until the spring of 1858. The church was organized October 11th, 1858, with twenty-nine members. The installation service of Dr. Rice as pastor was held in the Tenth Church, October 18th, and the sermon preached on that occasion by Dr. W. P. Breed was afterwards published in tract form by the Presbyterian Board of Publication. Dr. John McDowell delivered the charge to the pastor and Dr. Henry A. Boardman the charge to the people. Samuel H. Fulton and William D. Hoyt, M. D., were the first elders.

The number at the organization was 29; nine months later (June, 1859), the membership had increased to 42, and consisted of the

following persons : Charles Balbirnie, Mrs.
Margaret Balbirnie, Mrs. Elizabeth E. Basse-
ter, Mrs. Charlotte Broomell, Miss Elizabeth
N. Brown, Thomas Bryan, Mrs. Elizabeth
Bryan, Jared Craig, Mrs. Ann Craig, Mrs.
Nancy Cunningham, Miss Ellen N. Dickinson,
Mrs. Catharine Duffy, Samuel H. Fulton,
Mrs. Margaret Fulton, Mrs. Jessie Goodsman,
Miss Mary J. Gowen, William D. Hoyt, Mrs.
Eliza Kerr, Mrs. Gracie Keyser, Charles W.
Leavitt, Mrs. Susannah C. Lewis, Miss Marga-
ret Mahood, John Mason, Mrs. Margaret R.
Mason, Mrs Elizabeth McCormick, Miss
Eliza McCormick, James McFarland, Mrs.
Sarah McFarland, Samuel McMullen, Miss
Sarah McMullen, Miss Margaret J. McMullin,
Miss Mary E. McMullin, Miss Mary McWil-
liam, Miss Catharine C. Mink, Mrs. Margaret
Preston, Mrs. Elizabeth M. Rice, John M.
Rice, Mrs. Margaret Rivell, Miss Elizabeth
Rivell, Miss Isabella Smith, Mrs. Margaret
Taylor, Mrs. Anna C. Thompson, Robert
Vincent.

There were 180 male scholars, 249 female
scholars, 14 male teachers and 16 female
teachers—making a total Sunday-school membership of 459.

The pastor held monthly afternoon meetings
for the training and instruction of those who
were considering the question of uniting with

the church. Much good resulted from this loving and painstaking attention.

Dr. Rice continued in charge of the church until October 15th, 1863. During his efficient ministry the church at one time numbered 110 members. When he resigned, the congregation passed very complimentary resolutions relative to his "untiring zeal and faithful ministry;" and the session of the Tenth Church put on record "their deep sense of the fidelity, ability, and unsparing labor with which their esteemed brother had discharged the duties of his pastorate, and their gratitude to God for the blessings which had attended his efforts."

After the departure of Dr. Rice, the school rapidly decreased in membership. The question of continuing the church was raised, and a committee appointed by Presbytery to investigate the matter made the following report :

" It is not believed by your committee that it would be either right or expedient for Presbytery to permit this church to remain in its present condition. It is without a pastor ; its income is small; and those who have for years been working for its increase and upbuilding are becoming discouraged. If it remains in its present unprogressive state it must necessarily decline and speedily become extinct. In this state of the case, but two methods, in the judgment of your committee, remain open :

" First.   The church may be dissolved, and
its members distributed to adjacent churches.
There will then nothing remain but a mission
school of the Tenth Church, to be supported
and controlled by that church.   The responsibility of the Presbytery in the matter will have
wholly ceased.

" Second.   The Presbytery may continue
the organization, and take measures to give
it increased efficiency, and augment its power
for doing good."

The report then gives in detail the difficulties in the way of adopting the latter course:
the narrow street in which the church is situated ; the chances of little or no improvement
in the neighborhood ; the unsuitability of the
present building for church purposes, and the
location of an attractive Presbyterian church
of the New School Branch within three squares
(Ninth and Wharton streets), with a flourishing school, against which it would seem almost
hopeless to compete.   To escape these disad-
vantages, the committee suggests that the
church be removed to another neighborhood
and assisted in the erection of a suitable building; and, further, that the location selected be
to the south and east of Broad street and
Washington avenue.   The report thus continues :

" The question which is thus raised might

be easily settled if the Moyamensing Church
and its property were wholly under the control
of the Presbytery, but this is not the case.
The Tenth Presbyterian Church originated
the Moyamensing Church by establishing
there a mission Sabbath-school, and by nobly
and generously supporting the church after its
organization. Some of the members of that
church are trustees of the Moyamensing
Church, and hold the titles of that property
in their names. The Presbytery, therefore,
can do nothing without a full and fraternal
consultation with the pastor and session of the
Tenth Church, and with those gentlemen of
that church who hold the legal title to the
church building of the Moyamensing Church.
In order that this may be accomplished, your
committee would respectfully suggest the pas-
sage of the following resolution :

" *Resolved :* That a copy of this report be
transmitted to the session of the Tenth Church
and that the session be requested to furnish
Presbytery at an early date with a statement
of their views and wishes in regard to the matter submitted in this report."

In a paper dated October 1, 1864, written
by Dr. Boardman, the session of the Tenth
Church thus makes answer :

" The session of the Tenth Church, having
duly considered the paper referred to them

by the Presbytery of Philadelphia, respectfully submits the following reply :

"It is now twenty-two years since the Tenth Church established a mission school in Moyamensing ; and six years since a church was organized there. In both its forms, as a school and as a church, the enterprise was blessed of God. We believe it will be be said of many ransomed sinners at the last day, 'This and that man was born there.'

"Under the ministry of a faithful and laborious pastor, aided by a most efficient corps of teachers, an interesting church was collected, comprising a very goodly number of active, working Christians. It became apparent, however, to all concerned, that the neighborhood was one in which no *self-supporting church* could be built up, and that the utmost exertions of all engaged in the effort would be requisite to maintain the status of the congregation already secured. By the course of events, several of the most zealous and influential of the Christian men, who, without (in some cases), becoming communicants there, had given their time and labors to the enterprise, were obliged to remove to other and distant churches. After this, the school sustained a serious loss in the withdrawal of several of the stated teachers ; and finally, their excellent pastor felt it to be his duty to resign his charge and seek another field of labor.

" These events could not fail to operate disastrously upon a church situated like this one, the more so as circumstances occurred which augmented their untoward influence. These circumstances, it could do no good to relate. Enough that the misfortunes that have overtaken that promising mission, are attributable *in no form or degree* to us as a session, or to the church we represent, for even the falling off in the annual subscriptions of our congregation to this mission was only an effect resulting from causes beyond their control.

" We are aware that harsh judgments have been pronounced upon the session of the Tenth Church for their supposed delinquencies in this matter. We are not careful to repel these censures ; they spring more from ignorance than malice. They will find slight countenance among the excellent people of the Moyamensing Church. They *know* that the Tenth Church has testified its concern for their welfare by tokens of regard not to be mistaken. They must be assured that they have our hearty sympathy in their present trials, and that we would do anything in our power which a wise and prudent policy would dictate, to succor them.

" To build them a *new church edifice* is not,

and never has been, in our power. We have always hoped that they might grow into a self-sustaining church, and that through a general effort on the part of the churches of our Presbytery, they might one day be put in possession of a suitable house of worship. It would appear from the report referred to us, that the Presbytery regard this time as having come, and that all that is necessary to accomplish the object is a transfer to the Moyamensing Church of the lot and building they now occupy (free of rent), and the title to which is in the Board of Trustees of the Tenth Church.

" Assuredly our church is the last one in the Presbytery which would in any way hinder the attainment of so desirable an end—it is what we have been longing for these twenty-two years. During this entire period, the enterprise, first as a Sunday-school, then as a church, has derived its chief pecuniary support from our congregation. We claim no merit for what we have done. It was not less our pleasure than our duty. Nor do we speak of it in this place willingly, but the occasion seems to require of us the simple statement that eighteen or twenty thousand dollars would, in our judgment, be a fair estimate of the amount contributed by the Tenth Church for the culture of this mission-field. We wish the sum had been still larger. We are con-

vinced that the seed thus sown has, by God's
blessing, yielded a harvest which is above all
price, and we think the fact ought to satisfy
all parties, that we cannot be indifferent to the
future fortunes of this mission.

"The Presbytery, of course, would not wish
us to *imperil* the Moyamensing property. Its
financial value is not great, for it is incum-
bered with a mortgage of $1,000. But such
as it is, we have no moral right to expose it
to those hazards which have proven fatal to
the property of so many of our feeble churches.
Should the building cease to be required for
worship by the Moyamensing Church, that is,
should this church be forced by uncontrollable
circumstances to relinquish its organization,
the Tenth Church would still be bound to use
the property, or its avails, for the objects contemplated in the original subscription. But
if the Moyamensing Church shall, within
two years from this time, secure funds sufficient to pay for a lot, and erect, free of debt, a
suitable church edifice—sufficient, *i. e.*, when
supplemented by the avails of the property
they now occupy—we agree on behalf of the
trustees and session of the Tenth Church, that
the property in question, or the proceeds
thereof, shall be made over to them.

"We suppose that this offer covers the
ground contemplated in the report referred to

us. We think it is every thing which the struggling Moyamensing Church or the Presbytery could ask of us. And we trust that both the church and the Presbytery will see in it another evidence of our deep and abiding interest in the well-being of that congregation and the prosperity of our cause in the southern part of the city.''

The Presbytery on October 3d, 1864, took the following action :

'' *Resolved*, That the report submitted by the session of the Tenth Church in the matter of the Moyamensing Church, is highly satisfactory to this Presbytery and the proposition contained in the report is one honorable to that church, and entirely acceptable to this body.''

The plan to continue the church was found impracticable, however, and on October 13th, Presbytery took the following action :

''*Resolved*, That the Moyamensing Church be, and it is hereby dissolved, and the members thereof be recommended to connect themselves with neighboring churches.''

The Rev. Dr. Matthew B. Grier was appointed to announce this action to the members of the Moyamensing Church ; he was also appointed by Presbytery to give, in conjunction with the session of the church, certificates of dismission to the members. The *school*, however, was continued.

A CRITICAL PERIOD

The following paper, written in January, 1899, by Dr. S. T. Lowrie, gives an interesting glimpse of the field in 1864-5:

"I visited Philadelphia in August, 1864, to learn whether I could be employed here in some work of church extension. The Presbytery of Philadelphia had a committee to look after such enterprises. It consisted of the Rev. Dr. M. B. Grier, (who died Jan. 23d, 1899), the Rev. F. Reck Harbaugh and Mr. John Harper, and my inquiries brought me into communication with them. This, be it remembered, was before the Reunion. It was not plain to the committee that Presbytery could accept my offer of service, but they thought my services would be acceptable in the Carpenter Street Mission of the Tenth Church—also called the Moyamensing Mission —and undertook to arrange that. As the Presbytery would not meet before October, the committee could not earlier present this matter for its action.

"Thus it came to pass that in October, 1864,.

I returned to Philadelphia and began work in the Moyamensing quarter as a missionary of the Presbytery, with the Moyamensing Sabbath-school of the Tenth Church as the basis of operation. After a little acquaintance with the region, I found a lodging on Ninth street, not far from the school, and lived in the field I was to cultivate.

" The church that had existed under Dr. W. M. Rice, having been dissolved, and the greater part of the members having been enrolled in the Tenth Church that fostered the mission Sabbath-school, there could be no meetings there on Sunday mornings, for the people who could make a congregation owed attendance at the Tenth Church. But there was the Sabbath-school in the afternoon; and Sunday evening and Wednesday evening services were instituted there, and other house meetings held during the week. It was a hearty and happy work for all who were actually engaged in it. But the meetings continued small, and under any adversity were likely to fail altogether. One of the few notes I still have of that period records that I preached on Feb. 12, 1865, Sunday evening, to six adults and three children. The text was: Zech. 3: 2, ' Is not this a brand plucked out of the fire ? '

" The chief interest was in the Sabbath-school. Mr. H. W. Pitkin was superintendent

and conducted the school, and Miss E. N.
Brown was assistant superintendent. But after
a few months Mr. Pitkin was able to be there
only occasionally, so that I had often to conduct the school; and I was always teaching
classes for which no regular teachers could be
found. The teachers who were regular and
reliable were few; but they were very admirable for ability and devotion to their work, and
taught large classes. With such good workers and faithful work, it seemed that, sooner
or later, there must come enlargement in every
respect, and with it the revival of a church.

"It was not the discouragements of the field
that led to my removal from it, but the very
hopeful character of another field. In the
spring of the year 1865 the Bethany Mission
applied to Presbytery to be taken under its
care, with the request that I should be trans-
ferred to that field. The circumstances of the
two fields led Presbytery to make the change,
in which I very heartily acquiesced. It was
not to take effect until I had fulfilled the year
for which, as it was understood, I had been
appointed to labor in Moyamensing. The
year practically ended when the Carpenter
Street Sabbath-school reduced work for the
summer, as was necessitated by reason of the
teachers there being, nearly all of them, persons who lived out of the city in summer.

" But more than reduction of the school took place; for, in view of the discouragements attending the work, the session of the Tenth Church judged it expedient to discontinue the mission Sabbath-school. I was invited by Dr. H. A. Boardman, the pastor, to participate in the mournful transaction that was intended to conclude the efforts to plant a church by that mission. It took place, I think, in the afternoon of the last Sunday of June, (25th) 1865, with appropriate worship of God, recounting the blessings of the past and acquiescing in what seemed to be His present will.

" It was, however, not so to be. There were murmurs against the action of the session. Before the summer dispersion of the teachers of the school took place, consent was got by some of them to make a further trial. The prime movers in this were Miss Estabrook and Miss Penrose, and word was spread among the Sabbath-school scholars that the school would be opened again in October. What happened then and thereafter belongs to the first chapter of the inspiring story of the rise and progress of the Hollond Memorial Church.''

MISS ELLEN A. ESTABROOK

THE NEW LIFE

The Rev. Heber H. Beadle, now, and for the past thirty-three years, pastor of the Second Presbyterian Church, Bridgeton, N. J., has prepared the following paper on a very interesting and important period in the history of the school—the period immediately following that described by Dr. Lowrie in the preceding chapter:

"It was my good fortune to be connected with the Hollond Memorial field in days long past; it was my misfortune that it was only for a very short service. After a lapse of more than thirty years my recollections of it are somewhat indefinite and unsatisfactory.

"In the fall of 1865, after the church had been for some time disbanded and the school had been abandoned, when the work in that field seemed almost hopeless to all except a faithful few—like Miss Estabrook and Miss Lydia S. Penrose—I was asked by them to look over the field and see whether, in my opinion, something could not yet be done to restore life to what seemed to be most utterly dead.

"They talked the matter over with Mr. H. W. Pitkin, the former superintendent, and myself, and with such persistence and enthusiasm that we were made to believe that it was worth while, at least, to try to see what could be done—there might be a spark of life somewhere, which, by judicious nursing, would come to something.

" Being for the moment an idler in the market place, I was glad of an opportunity to work for Christ, even in so unpromising a field.

" One Sabbath in October we met in the school room with a few of the teachers of the old school and the matter was again talked over most earnestly and most prayerfully. It was finally determined that, if we could gain permission from the proper authorities in the mother church, we would re-open the school and see if a determined purpose, along with the help of God, would not bring the success which we coveted; and that the dead should be made to rise and walk.

" We did not wish to make an experiment— that had been done already—we wanted to *do* the thing. Notice was given at once, through the teachers and a few scholars who had come in to see what was to be done, that there would be school in that place the next Sunday and every Sunday thereafter; and that everybody was invited to come, and to bring others with them. In the meanwhile, Miss Estabrook, Miss Penrose and myself were to see the au-

MISS LYDIA S. PENROSE

thorities and win them over to let us have the building. Knowing well the good men who had the matter in charge, we did not anticipate any real difficulty.

" With two such brave, faithful, self-forgetting souls as these back of the enterprise, to suggest, to insist, to have heart and courage enough for all that had little or none, difficulties vanished and hope was born where there had been only despair before.

" We were allowed to try the 'experiment,' as it was called, but those who gave the permission gave it without the least faith in the world that any more would come of it than had already come—that is, absolute and pitiable failure. But we had other ideas, and were the more determined to make not failure but success of the trial, if God would help, and of that we had not the least doubt.

" The place was not a pleasant and cheerful one to which to invite children. An abandoned room is rarely a bright one. The benches were old, cut, and carved, broken and repaired by home talent; the walls were not very clean; the windows were almost as useful for ventilation as for light, and for the first we had no need whatever—the cracked and shrunken doors gave enough of that. During the week we went to a tailor's and bought a basket of list, and a large and heavy basket it was to carry, I remember. Borrowing a hammer and buying tacks, we went out to the school and spent the day in caulking up the rents and holes that let in too much of the winter air; and doing this and many other like things that much needed to be done, we succeeded in making the place warmer and more presentable for the children.

"Some of the teachers who had been faithful in the old school in spite of many discouragements, who stood ready again for still harder work, and who lived near by, agreed to have the room washed and cleaned for the next Sabbath. So much was done to the building.

"The neighborhood was visited, every child seen upon the street was smiled upon and asked to come to the school, and from the outset it was work, work, work, and pray, pray, pray, until to the amazement of all—save those whose hearts had been in the service—the school was set upon its feet, and began to grow strong in a way to delight those of us who had undertaken the work against the judgment of many much wiser than ourselves, and almost against our own most cherished hopes at the beginning.

"In the spring of 1866 I was called to take charge of the church where I am at present, and very reluctantly was compelled to give up the superintendency of the school that was

REV HEBER H. BEADLE

now growing so prosperous, into better hands
to carry on to new successes.

"Miss Estabrook and Miss Penrose were still,
as at first, the moving spirits that, under God,
furthered the work to its wonderful ultimate
growth. In the present unbarring of the
doors of the past to let in light by which to
see the faces of those who toiled so patiently,
so faithfully, and did so much, when there was
no promise for reward save in the promises of
God, and it was hoping against hope to remain
in that field, the names of these two faithful servants of God should not be overlooked;
for they were the very life of the effort.
Others took hold and toiled too, and with all
their hearts—most noble helpers they were,
and without them success would have been
impossible or much delayed—but about the
earnest, insistent, unwearying efforts of these
two did everything turn at the beginning, and
their names ought to be written upon a tablet
of bronze and set upon the walls of the church
—for without them it would not have been,
humanly speaking."

[Miss Estabrook is now (1899) living in
Barre, Mass. The devotion of Miss Penrose
to the work has continued through the years
and she is still one of the most valued teachers
of the school.]

INSPIRATION

" They helped every one his neighbor ; and every-
one said to his brother, Be of good courage." Isaiah
41 : 6.

The efforts of Mr. Beadle, Miss Penrose, Miss
Estabrook, and others were crowned with almost
unlooked-for blessings. Miss Harriet Hollond,
a prominent teacher in the Tenth Church,
expressed her great joy, and promised financial assistance. She had the walls whitewashed,
and the heater, which could only be relied on
to fill the room with smoke, put in good order.
Former teachers, catching the enthusiasm, returned to the work, and gathered in their scattered scholars. Hope was in every face, faith
and courage in every heart. There was a
swing and *go* about everything, and a mighty,
heaven-born impulse that was full of cheer and
inspiration for all. Three months later, Christmas was joyfully celebrated with *two hundred
scholars*.

Mr. A. B. Shearer was made superintendent,
and he was succeeded by the Hon. J. K. Findlay. In the early part of 1870, Judge Findlay

resigned, and the teachers unanimously elected Mr. Charles E. Morris, a promising young lawyer, and at that time a teacher in Bethany, to fill the vacancy. He declined to accept, but consented to become associate superintendent, provided Mr. Julian Cary would act as superintendent at the regular session of the school on Sunday afternoons, thus allowing Mr. Morris to meet his class in Bethany. This arrangement continued until the spring of 1871, when Mr. Cary removed to New York. Mr. Morris was again elected superintendent, and, to the great joy of the officers and teachers, accepted.

He held the important position with marked ability and success until his untimely death on the 10th of February, 1879. Under his magnetic leadership the school made great progress. The seats in the old Moyamensing building were replaced by better ones; the floor, which had given way during one of the sessions, was relaid; the house was repainted; the division wall between the main room and the infant school was removed, and new life and energy took the place of old and worn-out methods.

A few days before the death of Harriet Hollond, which occurred on the 9th of August, 1870, she added a codicil to her will, in which she bequeathed $10,000 to the Tenth Church, provided it would undertake, within five years, to place the Moyamensing school in a more desirable neighborhood.

The Tenth Church accepted the terms of Miss Hollond's legacy, and contributed an equal amount. On the 16th of June, 1873, it entered into a contract with Charles D. Supplee, architect, to erect a handsome memorial chapel.

The site finally selected was at the southwest corner of Federal and Clarion streets, the lot originally chosen, at Twelfth and Wharton streets, being relinquished.

Ground was broken June 17th, and the corner-stone laid July 31, 1873. The exercises were participated in by the Rev. Willard M. Rice, D.D., of the Fourth Presbyterian Church; the Rev. J. R. Miller, D. D., of the Bethany Presbyterian Church ; and the Rev. J. Henry Sharpe, D. D., of the Wharton Street Presby-

terian Church.   Mr. Charles E. Morris, superintendent, also took part.

The dedicatory services commenced on Sunday morning, February 15, 1874, the day being
an unusually beautiful one.   The Rev. Henry
A. Boardman, D. D., preached the opening sermon from the texts *"O Lord our God, all this
store that we have prepared to build thee an house
for thine holy name cometh of thine hand,
and is all thine own."*   1 Chron. : 29-16.

*"This also that she hath done, shall be spoken
of for a memorial of her."*   Mark 14 : 9.

Among other things, he said :

"This commodious and beautiful structure,
whose walls to-day resound for the first time
with the praises of Almighty God, is not pri-
marily designed as a church, but as a Sunday-
school mission chapel.   The predominant service is to be the careful religious training of the
young ; to be blended, however, with the
preaching of the Gospel, and its kindred exercises.

"You bring the Gospel to the very door of the
people.   You bring it to them without money
and without price, under circumstances which
leave no possible room for them to distrust the
purity of your motives.   You address yourselves to the young who are accessible to
the approaches of kindness, and who are the
particular objects of the Divine regard.   Your

whole aim concerning them is to rescue them from evil courses, to throw around them the only adequate safeguard against temptation, to make them wiser and better and happier, to fit them for the duties of this life, and the enjoyments of the life to come. The wholesome agency thus brought to bear upon the young, they carry into their homes. Children become missionaries to their parents; all the more efficient, because neither party recognizes the relation, and the healthful influence distills around silently like the dew. Intemperance, profaneness, and crime, will be checked; order, industry, and frugality will prevail, and you will have done more for the peace and thrift of the neighborhood, than the police could have accomplished in a score of years."

"But your aim is higher than personal reformation, or domestic comfort, or social order, or all of these combined. You come hither as to the lost, to make known to them a Saviour; you come to snatch deathless souls from endless ruin; you come to train perishing sinners for Heaven."

Of Miss Hollond, he said, in part: "With a humility never exceeded in any Christian of whom I have known or read, she shrank from hearing her name used in connection with any of her daily benefactions. Her ambition never rose beyond the privilege of ministering to the

relief, temporal and spiritual, of God's suffering poor, and for these ever-repeated offices of
kindness she would not hear without protest a
word of commendation even from her dearest
friends."

At 2 P. M., the Sunday-school assembled for
the last time in the old brick school-house on
Carpenter street. After a parting hymn and
prayer, they filed out by classes and marched
to the new chapel, singing "Our Sabbath
Home." The boys entered by the east door,
the girls by the west, and took their appointed class forms. "The little people of the
Infant and Primary rooms came last, and
when all were in place, Mr. Morris tapped his
bell, the singing ceased, all were simultaneously seated, and the exercises of the school went
on just as in the old hall." Mr. W. L. Cooke
made the opening prayer.

In the evening, the co-pastor of the Tenth
Church, the Rev. Louis R. Fox, preached.
The Rev. Willard M. Rice, D. D., also
spoke.

On Monday, the 16th, the Rev. Dr. S. T.
Lowrie, read the Scriptures and made the opening prayer. Addresses to the children were
delivered by the Rev. James M. Crowell, D. D.,
and J. Bennet Tyler, Esq. The following
original dedication hymn was sung:

Father, enthroned above,
Hear us in gracious love ;
  Accept our vows :
Holy and Sovereign Lord,
Keep Thou the watch and ward,
Be the perpetual Guard
  Of this Thy House.

Thou, the Anointed One,
God's own eternal Son,
  Grant us Thine aid :
Here let Thy favor dwell,
Here may Thy praises swell ;
Saviour, Immanuel,
  Be Thou our Head.

Oh, Holy Comforter,
Thy people, prone to err,
  Thy help implore :
Presence Divine, unseen,
Breathe every heart within,
Cleanse from all taint of sin,
  Forevermore.

Jehovah ! Lord and King,
Angels Thy glory sing
  Through endless days :
World without end, to Thee,
To Thy great Majesty,
Father, Son, Spirit, be
  Eternal praise !

A report was read by Mr. Charles E. Morris, showing that there had been a total expenditure of $30,000, all but $3,400 of which had been paid. $20,000 of the amount had come through the Tenth Church and Miss Hollond,

$4,000 from the sale of the old Carpenter street
building, and about $1,000 from the mite boxes
used by the children of the school. $70.00 of
this was raised by Miss Elizabeth Rivell's class.
In less than two weeks after the report was
made, the building, through the liberality of
two good friends of the school, was free from
debt.

On Tuesday, the 17th, the Rev. Henry C.
McCook, D. D., Hon. W. S. Peirce, Rev. E.
R. Beadle, D. D., of the Second Presbyterian
Church, and the Hon. John Wanamaker, took
part.

On Wednesday evening, the Rev. H. V. S.
Meyers, of New York, the Rev. W. W. Hallo-
way, of Jersey City, and the Rev. Wm. P.
Breed, D. D., of the West Spruce Street Presbyterian Church, were the speakers.

Thursday evening, the Rev. H. J. Van Dyke,
D. D., of Brooklyn, and the Rev. J. F. Dripps,
of Germantown, preached. On Friday evening, the sermon was delivered by the Rev. W.
W. Ormiston, D. D., of New York city. Saturday evening was observed as a praise and
thanksgiving service, in which the Rev. Dr.
Z. M. Humphrey, the Rev. Dr. J. R. Miller,
and Messrs. Maurice A. Wurts and James O.
McHenry participated.

At this time there were 36 officers and teachers, 55 primary scholars, 210 infant scholars,

and 222 scholars in the main room —making
a total of 523. The officers were: Charles E.
Morris, superintendent; William L. Cooke, associate superintendent; William L. Du Bois,
treasurer; Samuel R. Sharp, treasurer of memorial fund; Walter K. Maxwell and William
W. Porter, secretaries; Charles J. Cooke and
Robert Briggs, librarians.

At the dedication of the chapel the keys
were placed in the hands of Mr. James C.
Taylor, who was one of the early Moyamensing scholars and whose active interest in the
work still continues. Perhaps no member of
our church has ever been at heart more truly
devoted to its service or more closely identified
with it. To many of us his name and Hollond
are almost synonymous terms. Beginning life
with but few advantages he deserves special
credit for having won his way to the front
ranks of our city's painters. As a practical
business man, his experience and advice have
been of great value to our board of trustees,
of which body he is a member. He was one
of the loyal men who went to the front at their
country's call during the war of the rebellion
and he is justly proud of his record as a soldier.

The chapel is of Gothic architecture, and is
built of Trenton brown stone. It has a frontage of sixty-two feet on Federal street and

THE HOLLOND CHAPEL

ninety on Clarion. Two vestibules on Federal
street, ten feet square, give entrance to the
main room and to the galleries. The north
gallery was erected with the chapel; the two
side galleries were added in 1882. The library,
superintendents' room, secretaries' room, and
wash room, are at the north end of the building; four Bible class rooms are on the west
side and two on the east side, and the Primary
and Junior rooms are at the south end, back
of the pulpit platform. By means of slid-
ing glass partitions, all of these class rooms
can be at will opened on or separated from the
main audience room. The building is seated
with chairs, which can be arranged into class-
forms for Sunday-school purposes or placed in
rows for other services. The pulpit was the
gift of a Sunday-school class in Bethany, and
the organ, made and bought in Paris, was presented by a member of the Tenth Church.
The building has a total seating capacity of
above one thousand. Davis E. Supplee was
the supervising architect.

Many loving hearts have been, and are, interested in the beautiful stained glass windows
which adorn the chapel—each of them being a
memorial of a loved one gone. The committee
having charge of securing these windows were
much encouraged at the very beginning by receiving an offer of two windows from a lady

who had originally given them to a church in the interior of the State, from whence they were removed owing to a growing prejudice in that community against such memorials being erected in churches. These windows, which bear the names of Saul and Katherine Hood McCormick, were gladly accepted and are now among the most beautiful in the building. The two large front windows were donated by personal friends of Harriet Hollond. Among the names commemorated by some of the other windows are Rev. W. M. Engles, D.D., Mrs. Rebecca M. Schott, Emily Duncan, Ellen W. Jones, Dr. John MacDowell Rice, U. S. N., (presented by the Fourth Presbyterian Church) ; Hattie Wanamaker (presented by Grace Chapel, Jenkintown); Rev. Dudley A. Tyng; Rev. John Todd, D.D. (presented by the Clinton Street Presbyterian Church); John Cresswell; Rev. Albert Barnes (presented by the First Presbyterian Church); John Wilson (presented by the Woodland Presbyterian Church); Helen B. Glass, Benjamin John Cooke, Harvey Mann, Jr., Rachel J. Mann, James B. Mann, Mrs. Samuel Sharp, James B. McFarland and William Jardine.

Among the churches not mentioned above which presented windows were the old Tenth, Bethany, Chambers' and Cohocksink.

In the main room there are handsome tablets

to the memory of Harriet Hollond, Dr. Henry A. Boardman, and Charles E. Morris.

In 1875, steps were taken which resulted in the building of the cozy parlor over the Primary and Junior class rooms. The following description of the movement appeared in *Our Sabbath-School Helper* of April 11, 1875:

"Since the occupation of the Hollond Memorial Chapel the need of a room suitable for social and prayer meetings has been greatly felt. But remembering the prompt and generous contributions which gave us a beautiful and attractive chapel without a dollar of debt upon it, we chose rather to suffer the inconvenience than trespass further on the liberality of those who have done so much for us. Providence seems now to have opened the way for the accomplishment of this object. Miss Annie Morris, a beloved teacher in our school, whose recent death we so deeply lament, died possessed of a mortgage of $2000, to which by law, her parents, Mr. and Mrs. Morris, succeed. These parents, remembering that their daughter once offered this mortgage as a loan without interest for the completion of the chapel, and believing that it is a sacred trust, have been led to offer the money to the chapel, on condition that the balance required for the proposed addition be raised, so that no debt remain after the completion. The whole cost of the addition is estimated not to exceed $4,500."

The offer was accepted on the condition proposed. The work of building the addition was commenced May 28, 1875, and pushed forward with such vigor that it was completed September 23rd. Its total cost, including furniture and memorial window, was $5,000. The last $200.00 of this amount was obtained from a concert given by the scholars and some of their friends, February 15, 1876—the second anniversary of the dedication of the chapel. This pleasant " upper chamber " has been a great blessing. It is specially dear to many of the active workers of the church, for in it they have had precious and tender revealings of the Holy Spirit ; and many of our young people have there been inspired to make the first feeble efforts which have since led them onward to splendid Christian usefulness.

Miss Morris was the sister of Mr. Charles E. Morris, and had given valuable service to the school. Her memory is perpetuated by a beautiful tablet on the walls of the room which was made possible by the liberality and thoughtfulness of her parents. The beautiful window in the east end of the room is also a memorial of her.

Shortly after her death in March, 1875, an extended obituary notice, prepared by the Rev. H. J. Van Dyke, D.D., of Brooklyn, appeared in *The Presbyterian*, from which the following brief extracts are made:

"Her intellect was of a high order and was cultivated by habitual reading and study. Back of her social qualities, and infinitely more precious, there was a deep fountain of tenderness, and a well of living water springing up to everlasting life. The three characteristics of her religious life were supreme loyalty to Christ, love for the poor and lowly for His sake, and an intelligent devotion to the Presbyterian Church. These characteristics pervaded every part of her nature, and became more and more predominant. Her love for the poor and lowly was demonstrated during the last years of her life in her active zeal in connection, first, with the Bethany Mission, and afterwards with the Hollond Memorial Chapel. She had no fear of compromising her character or her position with ignorance and poverty. She was as ready to sing the songs of Zion in a hovel, or beside the bed of a dying child, as in the church or a parlor. To win the affectionate confidence of a class of rough boys was, in her eyes, a conquest worthy of her accomplishments."

The chapel remained the property of the old Tenth Church until the dissolution of that church in 1895, when it became, by gift of the mother church, the property of Hollond. The expense of maintaining the building was met by the Tenth Church, an annual appeal being sent to all the members for contributions. The following list, accidentally preserved, contains the names of those who contributed to this purpose for the year beginning October 1, 1876, and is here given to show the liberality of the members of the Tenth Church to the enterprise :

James Baird, $5.00; Mrs. Bayard, $100.00; Dr. Boardman, $25.00; Miss Mary Brown, $50.00; Misses Burt, $25.00; Cash, $25.00; Miss Chester, $75.00; Proceeds of concert at chapel, $72.25; Henry Cowan, $10.00; A. C. Craig, $10.00 ; John Crawford, $1.00 ; Dr. John DeWitt, $15.00 ; Dr. John Dickson, $25.00 ; W. E. DuBois, $10.00 ; W. L. DuBois, $25.00; Mrs. Z. Gemmill, $10.00; Mrs. J. R. Grier, $50.00; Mrs. M. Johnson, $25.00; Mrs. J. Kennedy, $2.00; Miss Mary S. Kirke, $20.00; Rev. W. W. Latta, $10.00; Mrs. Law, $5.00 ; Margaret MacMullen, $1.00 ; Mrs. Milliken $10.00; P. McBride, $25.00; Charles E. Morris, $35.co; Mrs. Penrose, $25.00; Mrs. A. K. Pomeroy, $25.00; W. W. Porter, $40.00; Mrs. Potts, $5.00; Miss E. Rogers, $2.00; Mrs. J. B. Ross, $100.00; Misses Sanford, $10.00; Mrs. Savage, $50.00; Miss Mary B. Smith, $150.00; Miss Margaret R. Smith, $50.00; Tenth Church collection, $125.13 ; Peter

Walker, $10.00; William Wilson, $50.00; Mr. White, $1.00; C. Wurts, $10.00; Young People's Association of Hollond Chapel, $9.30. Total, $1,308.68.

It should not be forgotten that this Appeal was sent out year after year, and always met with a generous response.

The Rev. Frederick B. Duval, a Princeton theological student, was in charge of the field during the summer of 1874. He returned to his studies in the fall. On the 12th of November, the Rev. William F. Garrett was ordained in the chapel as an evangelist to labor in connection with the mission. The Rev. S. W. Dana, D.D., acted as moderator, the Rev. William P. Breed, D.D., preached the sermon, the charge to the pastor was given by the Rev. Dr. Henry A. Boardman, and the address to the people by the Rev. J. M. Crowell, D.D.

In his report to the Tenth Church, May, 1876, Mr. Garrett thus writes: "The past year at the chapel has been one never to be forgotten, a year made sacred by the special advent and blessing of God in our very midst, by large additions to our church, by increased attendance at the services, by a quickening of Christians, and general interest in matters of religion.

"Preaching services have been conducted every Sabbath morning and evening; the aver-

age attendance in the morning being from two
hundred and fifty to three hundred, while in
the evening the attendance at times has numbered over five hundred. One hundred and
twenty-four persons have united with the
church. The Young People's Meeting on
Tuesday evenings has been blessed of God in
an especial manner, overflowing in attendance,
and characterized by fervency of spirit and the
energy of zeal. On Wednesday evenings cottage prayer-meetings have been held from
house to house. These meetings are conducted and sustained by the young men of the
chapel, who, having formed themselves into a
band of Christian workers, are unremitting in
their labors, having held as many as three or
more meetings during the week. The chapel
prayer-meeting is held every Friday night.
We cannot fully know here what the Holy
Ghost has done for us. Truly enough has
been accomplished to satisfy and amply repay
those who, in self-sacrifice, and love to Christ,
assisted to erect the Hollond Chapel; enough
has been done to make us thank God and
take courage.''

In his report made at the same time, Mr.
Charles E. Morris said: "It has been the
most eventful year of our history. Never
could so much be said of God's goodness and
mercy to us, and we have abundant cause for

thanksgiving and praise. Earnest prayers have been answered, long-cherished hopes realized, and the blessing richly poured upon us. Fifty-nine of our scholars have united with our church, and at least a score have joined other churches. We exclaim, ' Bless the Lord, O my soul, and forget not all his benefits!' ''

Mr. Morris also speaks of the good work accomplished by the young men's prayer-meeting, the cottage prayer-meeting, the mother's meeting, the young ladies' prayer-meeting, teachers' meeting, and the sewing school. In 1871, the school numbered 260; in 1874, 560; and in 1876, 925. In closing his report, Mr. Morris said: '' When the books shall be opened, and every secret thing be made known, it will be found that to Dr. Boardman, more than to any other human agency, has the success and present prosperity of our mission been due.''

The officers and teachers of the school at the time of this report (May, 1876), were: Charles E. Morris, superintendent; William L. Cooke and George C. McConnell, associate superintendents; William W. Porter, chorister; Walter K. Maxwell, W. J. Parry, Charles T. Cresswell, secretaries; Gustavus Harkness, Washington Freund, Hugh Kay, librarians.

Teachers: William B. Blight, Hon. T. B.

Dwight, Hon. John K. Findlay, Mrs. Sarah
G. Beck, Mrs. Samuel C. Hayes, Miss Eliza-
beth Potts, Miss Mary Potts, John L. Kugler,
Miss Mary Irvine, Miss Emma Fithian, Miss
Sallie Cooke, Mrs. Charles J. Cooke, Samuel
Cowan, William L. DuBois, Nathan H.
Jarman, Samuel M. Kennedy, Henry W.
Lambirth, John A. Martin, George C. Mc-
Connell, William H. Sivel, Samuel R. Sharp,
Mrs. Susan O. Babbitt, Mrs. Mary J. Boyd,
Miss Sallie Bunting, Miss Bessie Cooke,
Miss Jennie Cowan, Miss Lizzie Cresswell,
Miss Ellen Dickinson, Miss Lizzie Dukes,
Miss Mattie Fisher, Miss Lizzie C. Fithian,
Miss Mary R. Fox, Miss L. J. Gaskill, Miss
Sue A. Gaskill, Mrs. Ollie Y. Hamilton, Miss
Virginia F. Handy, Mrs. Clementine A.
Harper, Miss Hattie G. Henry, Miss Mary E.
Hill, Miss Cecelia Hogan, Miss Ella P. Irwin,
Miss Mary J. Kennedy, Miss Ellie S. Maxwell,
Miss Lily M. McBride, Miss Annie J. Mc-
Cormick, Miss Mary McCormick, Miss Jennie
C. McKane, Mrs. William E. Morris, Miss
Helen Parry, Miss Eleanor C. Patterson, Miss
Lydia S. Penrose, Miss Mary L. Pleasants,
Mrs. Anna K. Pomeroy, Miss Kate E. Reese,
Miss Elizabeth Rivell, Miss Eliza R. Sharp,
Miss Margaret R. Smith, Miss Lucie Stitt,
Miss Addie L. Stewart, Mrs. John L. Stewart,
Miss Annie Weaver.

Mr. Garrett resigned in the spring of 1878, and was succeeded by the Rev. J. Henry Sharpe, D.D.

Soon after this the school was called upon to sustain one of the most serious losses that could possibly come to it—the removal by death of its beloved superintendent, Mr. Charles E. Morris.

Dr. Louis F. Benson, his brother-in-law, thus writes of this untimely event: "His robust system had never wholly recovered from the effects of an attack of typhoid fever, and finally, after a hard battle, with the indomitable bravery of his spirit, it succumbed to the hand of disease; and in the endurance of pain and weakness, such as only he fully realized, his great soul went home by the thorny road of suffering, whereupon were the footprints and the helping hand of his Master. He died at seven o'clock on the morning of Monday, the 10th of February, 1879, at his residence in Spruce street, having been confined to his bed only since the Saturday evening preceding."

In his successor, Mr. Robert C. Ogden, the school was exceptionally fortunate in finding one whose practical experience, ripe judgment, and large-hearted liberality specially fitted him for so important a position. Under his wise superintendency, continued for a period of nearly twenty years, the school steadily advanced in numbers and in usefulness.

FAITH MISSION

The cottage prayer-meetings and other mid-week meetings which had been carried on so successfully by the young men of Hollond during the winter of 1875-6, had results little dreamed of at the time. As usual with all true spiritual service, not only were others helped but the workers themselves were inspired with fresh missionary zeal to win souls for the Master. Three active young men of the school felt that there was near at hand a wider field of usefulness which they might enter. On the 28th of December, 1876, these young workers—George C. McConnell, John L. Kugler and Edgar A. Leslie—had a meeting and resolved to canvass the neighborhood south of Dickinson street, and east of Broad, with a view of establishing a mission. They consulted with Mr. H. A. Brainard, an enthusiastic worker who had some experience in similar efforts, and from him and others they received such encouragement that on the 4th of January, 1877, they came before the teachers of Hollond to ask for their endorsement of the movement and for their support in meeting the rent of two small rooms at 1639 Passyunk avenue, which they had already secured, and in which they contemplated organizing a mission school. This support being readily and heartily promised, the young men went to work with a will to get the people of the immediate neighborhood interested in the movement, and with such success that when the school was opened on the 14th of January forty-five scholars and fifteen adults were present, eleven of the latter being there to engage in the work as teachers.

It was intended to call the new enterprise the Morris Mission, in honor of Mr. Charles E. Morris, but Mr. Morris objecting, the name Faith was substituted. The desk used was from the old Moyamensing school.

The school increased to such an extent during the next few Sundays, that at the February meeting of the Hollond teachers a report was made of the over-crowded condition of the rooms, and a committee was appointed to secure larger accommodations. An eligible site for a building was selected on the south side of Castle avenue, east of Broad, the price being $2,250. The land was taken on ground-rent. Hollond at that time not being a corporate body, could not take title to the ground but this was vested in twelve of the Hollond teach-

ers who thus became responsible for the principal and interest. The interest, amounting
to $135.00 annually, was paid from the Hollond
school fund from May, 1877, to April, 1882,
when the principal was paid by members of
the Tenth Church.

Mr. George C. McConnell, who was devoted
to the work, as chairman of the committee on
building purchased at auction sale February
12, 1877, one of the buildings which had been
used as police headquarters during the Centennial. The price paid was $200.00. He went
immediately after to the law office of Mr.
Morris, and the following petition was drawn
up:

"Being assured of the great necessity for
mission work directly south of the Hollond
Memorial Chapel, a number of earnest Christians, acting under the advice of the teachers
of our Hollond Memorial School, have organized a school to be known as Faith Mission.
The enterprise has in attendance exceeded our
expectations, and has made it necessary that
we should have a building better suited to our
wants. We have therefore purchased a frame
building, 36 by 70 feet, which will be erected
on Castle avenue, below Broad street, and will
cost, when completed, from $700.00 to $800.00.
In bringing this work to the attention of our
friends, we hope that many will feel willing to

aid us in the effort to establish a Presbyterian enterprise in a locality where it is greatly needed.''

To this appeal Mr. Morris was the first subscriber, and before noon the next day Mr. McConnell had succeeded in raising enough money to meet the first cost of the building. The expenditure, including the original cost, removal, erection on the new site, and general fitting up, was $1,861.94, nearly all of which, owing to the indefatigable efforts of Mr. McConnell, who was heartily assisted by the officers and teachers of Hollond, was paid within a year. The entire amount was paid in 1879. The teachers themselves gave much time and labor to make the building attractive and comfortable.

It was long the custom of Hollond to march up to the old Tenth Church on '' Anniversary Day.'' In May, 1877, ''Little Faith also marched up for the first time and from the gallery seats captured the hearts of all present by their enthusiastic singing of ' A better day is coming.' ''

In his printed report of the two schools— Hollond and Faith—in May, 1878, Mr. Morris said: ''Faith Mission is in reality a part of the work of the Hollond Memorial School.'' The officers and teachers at this time were: Superintendent, George C. McConnell; associate,

John L. Kugler; secretaries, Edgar A. Leslie and Jay F. Bryant; librarians, Joseph Young and George Taylor; teachers, Miss Emma Bryant, Miss Kate Roberts, Miss Maggie Henry, Mrs. L. Gibson, Miss A. J. Markfield, Miss Lizzie Osmond, Miss Lizzie Orr, Miss Mary Parvin, Miss Annie R. Patterson, Miss Minnie Sherwood, H. A. Brainard, Charles A. Chew, Charles Cook, George Douglass, W. H. Lamb, A. W. Martin, Charles A. Oliver, Samuel Patrick and Samuel Williamson. Sixteen of these were from Hollond. Mr. McConnell held the position of superintendent until his removal to San Francisco in 1884.

The new building was dedicated May 13th, 1877, at 4 o'clock, P. M. Addresses were made by Dr. Henry A. Boardman, Dr. John DeWitt, Rev. W. F. Garrett, Dr. J. Henry Sharpe, Hon. W. S. Pierce and Mr. Charles E. Morris.

In the spring of 1883 the mission was organized into the South Broad Street Presbyterian Church, and the Rev. J. C. Thompson, D.D., who had been successfully laboring in the field since 1880, was installed as the first pastor. In 1884 the organization was merged with and became known as the Scots Presbyterian Church. In 1888 the united congregations erected on the southeast corner of Broad street and Castle avenue one of the prettiest church buildings in the city. The old chapel is still in use as a Sunday-school room. Under the pastoral care of the Rev. George Handy Wailes, who was installed in 1897, this prosperous church is doing a noble work for the Master. The Hollond Church takes a pardonable pride in its advancement and prays for it the Father's richest blessings.

A PASTOR'S RECOLLECTIONS

[In the following paper the Rev. J. Henry Sharpe, D.D., now pastor of the West Park Church, Philadelphia, has kindly written of his connection with the Hollond field; and also of his impressions of some of the workers]:

At the Christmas holidays of 1870, Mr. John Wanamaker was unable to keep his engagement to speak at the festival of the Sabbath-school of the Wharton Street Church, of which I had recently become pastor, but he recommended in his place Mr. Charles E. Morris, a young lawyer, then in charge of a Bible class in the Bethany school. As a young pastor, the impression made on me by Mr. Morris' address on that occasion was strong and vivid; it abides with me to this day as characteristic of the vigorous and magnetic qualities I afterward learned to appreciate so highly by personal association with him in Sabbath-school work. He illustrated the moral of his address by the story of a boy who was following his father by treading closely in his footsteps through a blinding snow-storm at night. He was tempted to turn aside, thereby floundering into a deep drift from which he was rescued by his father at the last moment. The story was so told that it was impossible to forget it or its lessons. From that occasion I date my deep admiration for Charles E. Morris as the peer of the foremost Sabbath-school men I have known.

Another of the future makers and workers of Hollond I met two years later on the occasion of his installation as associate pastor of the Tenth Church. On the evening of January 25th, 1872, being then moderator of the Presbytery of Philadelphia, I was invited by Dr. Boardman to dine with him and meet his associate-elect, Rev. Louis R. Fox, and others, and proceed with them to the church at the hour of installation. Dr. Boardman preached the sermon, Dr. Breed charged the pastor, and Dr. Crowell charged the people. It was to me a memorable meeting with two men, a father and a brother, with both of whom I was thenceforward to sustain the most agreeable relations; becoming, in time, to be the associate of the one and the successor of the other.

A still later contact with these three strong friends of Hollond—Dr. Boardman, Mr. Fox and Mr. Morris—was in a friendly difference of opinion as to the wisdom of fixing the site of the proposed Hollond Memorial at Twelfth and Wharton streets, within three squares of

REV. J. HENRY SHARPE, D. D.

the Wharton Street Church. The Moyamensing Mission was first in the general field, and
so had a show of right to occupy any site
within it. The Presbytery, however, sided with
the protest of the Wharton Street Church, so
the Tenth Church sold its lot and selected the
present location of the Hollond Chapel. In
the light of subsequent events, all concerned
now see in this change of plan an overruling
providence, without which the wonderful after
development of the project could scarcely have
been possible.

It was a long step nearer Hollond when the
session of the Tenth Church, in the autumn
of 1874, extended to me an invitation to become the associate and assistant of Dr. Boardman, after the retirement of Mr. Fox from
that position. In the meanwhile, the Hollond
Chapel had been reared, and under the able
leadership of Mr. Morris, sustained by the
hearty co-operation of both the pastors of the
parent church, and under the immediate ministry successively of Mr. Duval and Mr. Garrett,
who had charge of the chapel services of worship, a large and growing school and also a
large and growing congregation were established. The prosperity of the mission pres-
ently became a source of embarrassment, as it
brought to consideration the propriety of separate and independent organization as a church.

It was natural that there should be honest and earnest differences of opinion on this subject. In his impassioned advocacy of what manifestly was premature as to time, ways, and means, Mr. Garrett withdrew from the mission and many of his sympathizers were ready to do the same. It was at this critical juncture of the history of Hollond that my own relations with it became most intimate.

I had been associate pastor with Dr. Boardman for nearly two years, when he felt constrained to resign his pastorate of more than forty years of continuous service. I presented my own resignation at the same time, and shortly afterwards accepted charge of the Gethsemane Mission of the Bethany Church at Point Breeze. Rev. Dr. John DeWitt became the successor of Dr. Boardman, and, like him, took a deep interest in the welfare of the Hollond Chapel.

When the vexed problem of independent organization at Hollond arose, as it did a year or so later, and Mr. Garrett had withdrawn, it was thought by Mr. Morris and his fellow teachers that one who understood the situation so thoroughly as I did might be helpful; accordingly the Tenth Church session, on petition of Mr. Morris and his corps of helpers, extended a call to me to come to the chapel as minister in charge.

My acceptance and installation (the latter taking place March 24th, 1878—Drs. DeWitt, Dulles and Crowell participating) brought me once more into fellowship with the Tenth Church flock, and especially with its earnest and enthusiastic group of workers at the Hollond Chapel. My providential relations were such as permitted and enabled me to do something in promoting mutual good understanding between the mother church and the mission. The question of organization was kept in abeyance, and the wisdom of this was seen in the rapid subsequent growth of both the school and the congregation worshipping in the chapel.

It was during this period that I was thrown into intimate association with Mr. Morris, the soul of the new Harriet Hollond Chapel. He had a large and thoroughly devoted company of co-laborers, and with their help he laid broad and deep foundations for the future. He builded better than he knew, for even he in those days had no vision of the great and grand church which was so soon to rise upon them. At the head of the whole enterprise, gathering about him kindred enthusiastic helpers, proposing and promoting every means to develop the usefulness of the mission, devising and co-operating with the establishment of Faith Mission, to the southward, for the overflow of the surplus energy and enterprise of the prosperous Hollond school and congregation, he made full proof of his calling and lifted the Hollond Memorial from obscurity to be one of the foremost as well as most promising fields in the southern section of the city.

As I review the past, it seems almost incredible that so much was accomplished under his brief administration. He was not spared to build on his own foundation or to reap where he had sowed, but the success of his labors was such that even he could not resist the lesson of expansion and manifest destiny. What he might have done had he lived out "the residue of his years," we shall never know. His work was limited to foundation laying, but therein he proved himself a master-builder. Before his seemingly untimely death he foresaw that Hollond could not remain a mission and must become a church. Had he lived he would doubtless have become a foremost spirit in converting the noble chapel into the nobler church and in consecrating it to the beneficent future, on which already it has so largely entered.

God called him away to an early reward, and those of us who were then identified with the mission were left broken-hearted, leaderless and almost hopeless. But God never calls away one workman before he has another

ready to take up his work. Mr. Morris was
followed by Mr. Robert C. Ogden, who, though
a recent resident of the city, had been trained
in similar work in Brooklyn and brought the
best methods of enlarged business and philan-
thropic experience to the wide and promising
field of the Hollond Memorial Mission. The
result was inevitable, if not immediately manifest. The prosperity of the enterprise rendered it impossible that it should remain a
mission, and in due season the parent church
not only acquiesced in the separate organization of the Hollond Memorial Church, but be-
stowed on the daughter her hearty benediction
in her independent establishment.

But before this was accomplished, the problems of the early transition period were too
various and trying for a pastor who was bound
by his office to be a mediator rather than an
advocate for either side. In withdrawing from
the Hollond Mission (Dec. 5th, 1880), I ex-
changed fields with another worker who was
destined to remain with the Hollond Memorial
for nearly a score of years thereafter. Rev.
Dr. J. R. Miller, who had long been the honored pastor of Bethany, was then the temporary supply of the West Park Church, which
called me to its pastorate. Beginning each his
new work within a few days of the other, it
has been my privilege to look on and witness

the wondrous growth of Hollond under the pastorate of Drs. Paden and Miller, and the superintendency of Messrs. Ogden and Cooke, and to rejoice in the ever-increasing prosperity of her whose praise is in all the churches. Though Morris and Ogden, and Paden and Miller are withdrawn, Martin and Overman, Cooke and Walker, and a goodly host of others, both men and women, remain—some of them unfaltering supporters of the work since the old Moyamensing days, their youth renewed with the immortal vigor of the new Hollond. It is the prayer alike of the old friends of Hollond and of the new, that "the glory of this latter house shall be greater than the former!"

The session of the Tenth Church took the following action on Mr. Sharpe's resignation: "(1). In accepting with great regret the resignation of Mr. Sharpe we desire to give expression to our sense of the great loss which the work at the Harriet Hollond Chapel will sustain in his removal. (2). We note also the great ability and fidelity with which Mr. Sharpe has carried forward his labors, and record our gratitude to God for the success which has followed them."

H. P. F.

We now enter upon the more modern era of our history—the era of church organization and of church building. Our foundations had been carefully and securely laid along broad and far-extending lines. The old Tenth had faithfully and lovingly nurtured her child, and now that child, in the full bloom of youthful vigor, was herself to assume churchly dignity and to launch forth as an independent organization—independent, yet clinging with never-ceasing trust and affection to the dear old mother church through which she had had her being, and from which, to the very last, she continued to receive direct and practical evidences of love and confidence.

As has already been shown, earnest men and women had made many personal sacrifices in order that the work might go on, and in its ever-increasing prosperity they had found much of encouragement and cheer. Now new leaders were to come to the front and to see to it that there should be no backward steps taken, no falling away from the high standards which had been so long maintained. Under the inspiration of a Miller, a Paden, an Ogden and a Cooke, the youthful church organization was to get the mighty impulse which was to sweep it from the newest and lowliest to the very front ranks of our city churches, and which was to raise it from an almost unknown mission station to an enviable position of far-reaching spiritual power and usefulness. Loyal men and women, many of them already long and faithful workers in the field, were to rally with renewed zeal about these leaders and to give to them the help and encouragement without which the ablest must fail.   Moses had Aaron and Hur to hold up his hands when the battle was going against his people, and successful men from that day to this have not gained their victories by fighting alone, for somewhere faithful hearts have struggled for them and with them and helped them to the winning. Our beloved church has been no exception. Our leaders have been successful largely because of the brave-hearted workers they have had to cheer and to support them.

Dr. J. R. Miller succeeded Dr. Sharpe.   He preached his first sermon in the chapel on the 2d day of January, 1881. His first letter to his new charge contained suggestions which were faithfully followed, and which not only gave to the work many of its distinctive feat-

REV. J. R. MILLER, D. D.

ures, but were also largely instrumental in giving the right impulse to much of its subsequent development. He wrote, in part :

"You can help to make this chapel a warm, loving place, into which the weary, the sorrowing, the poor, the friendless and the stranger will love to come. It costs but little to be kind, to reach out a cordial hand, to speak a few welcoming words ; and yet whole families have been won by just such simple courtesies in church aisles. Do not wait for introductions. Those who enter our church doors are our guests, and we must make them feel at home.

"I desire to have a place in your confidence, and in your affections. The work of a true pastor is more, far more, than the faithful preaching of the Word. He is a physician of souls, and his work must be largely personal. I desire, therefore, to become the close, personal friend of every one. I invite you to come to me freely for counsel and prayer in every matter that may concern your spiritual welfare. In sickness I want you to send for me. If you are in trouble, I claim the privilege of sharing it with you. I shall ever have a warm, ready sympathy, and a brother's helping hand for each of you when any burden presses, or any sorrow tries you. And in turn, I ask from you continual prayer, large patience, the firmest, truest friendship, a place in each home and heart, and ready co-operation in all the Master's work.

"Shall we not, one and all, sink every personal consideration and consecrate ourselves to a service for Christ and for souls, which shall only cease when we are called home to our rest and reward?"

This letter, as will be seen, would serve quite as fully to sum up Dr. Miller's work at the close of his long and helpful connection with our church as it did to outline it at the beginning.

The deep, spiritual current which was to flow so long and so prosperously now set in. "The people had a mind to work." It soon became evident that the time had come to organize the mission into an independent church. This action was determined upon at a congregational meeting held in the chapel on Friday evening, February 24th, 1882, when, on motion of Mr. Charles Hunter, it was

"*Resolved*, That a petition be signed by the members of the congregation, requesting the Presbytery of Philadelphia to grant the request for our organization into the Harriet Hollond Memorial Presbyterian Church of Philadelphia; and that the application be made through the session of the Tenth Presbyterian Church."

The following communication, received

through Mr. William L. DuBois from Dr. John DeWitt, pastor of the Tenth Church, was read. It is preserved here to show the feeling of the mother church in relation to the proposed action :

" It is not impossible that I shall be unable to attend the meeting of the Hollond Memorial congregation on February 24th. If I am not there, and it should seem to you to be well to say so, please state that I shall bid the new church God-speed most heartily ; and that I cannot believe that the Tenth Church's interest in the Hollond Memorial will be diminished in the slightest degree by the organization ; on the other hand, I believe that that interest will be increased."

A committee, consisting of Messrs. Robert C. Ogden, Theodore H. Loder, Charles Hunter, and William L. Cooke, was appointed to represent the congregation at the next meeting of Presbytery.

One month later, March 24th, 1882, the church was organized by a committee of the Presbytery, which consisted of Rev. Willard M. Rice, D.D., William L. DuBois and John Wanamaker, with General Stewart, John K. Findlay and Dr. J. R. Miller as corresponding members. The meeting was held in the chapel, Dr. Rice presiding. After brief devotional exercises, Dr. Miller read the names of the

228 members received from the Tenth Church, and of the one (Bates J. Griswold) received on profession of faith,—a total of 229 members for the new Hollond organization.

The following officers were elected by a rising vote : Elders—Robert C. Ogden, William L. Cooke, Samuel M. Kennedy, and Theodore H. Loder. Deacons—Charles Hunter, Alfred Adams, Charles A. Oliver, and Walter W. Reynolds. Dr. J. R. Miller received the unanimous call of the congregation to the pastorate. Addresses were made by Dr. Rice, Dr. DeWitt, Mr. W. L. DuBois, General Stewart, Judge Findlay, and Mr. John Wanamaker.

The church had no trustees until January 5th, 1883, when the following were elected : Robert C. Ogden, Theodore H. Loder, David Orr, James C. Taylor, Amos Dotterer, Henry A. Walker, John K. Findlay, William L. Cooke and James M. Leo.

The following list contains the names of the 229 persons who joined the church at its organization :

Alfred Adams, Mrs. Martha Adams, Miss Millie Allen, Mrs. Anna Auld.

Mrs. Eliza Bell, Miss Ella E. Biddle, Mrs. Louisa Bishop, Henry Bowman, Miss Agnes Boyd, Mrs. Elizabeth Boyer, Miss Mamie E. Brinton, Miss Mattie S. Brinton, H. Ernest Brown, Mrs. Lavinia Brown, Miss Mary Brulard, Mrs. Martha Bryant, Mrs. Hannah Bryant, Miss Emma Bryant.

Miss Mary J. Calder, William F. Campbell, Mrs. Anna Campbell, Miss Sadie Campbell, Mrs. Eliza Campbell, Miss Jennie Campbell, James Carnes, Mrs. Eliza Carnes, John Carson, Mrs. Jane Carson, Miss Florence A. Chalker, Mrs. M. Chestnut, Charles A. Chew, Miss Selena Chew, Miss Nellie Christie, Mrs. Susan Coates, Robert H. Cochran, Mrs. M. Cochran, Miss Mary J. Colwell, Miss Emma Coogan, Miss Mary Coogan, William L. Cooke, Miss Bessie Cooke, Miss Josie Cooke, Miss Carrie M. Craig, John Crosgrave, Mrs. John Crosgrave, Miss Sarah Crosgrave, Miss Jennie Crosgrave, Mrs. A. E. Cunningham, Mrs. W. S. Cunningham.

Miss Anna Louise Daly, Miss Priscilla Daly, Miss Katie Davis, Mrs. Lizzie Dos Passos, George Douglass.

Frederick Edwards, Mrs. Elizabeth Edwards, Mrs. Louisa Edwards, Mrs. Mary Elliott, Mrs. Mary Ellis.

Mrs. A. H. Fillott, Miss Fannie B. Fithian, Mrs. Anna Fleming, Miss Mary Fleming, Miss Sadie Fleming, Samuel Frame, Mrs. Mary Frame.

Mrs. Annie Gallagher, Mrs. Elizabeth Gamble, Miss Lizzie Gamble, Mrs. Laura Gardner, Mrs. Virginia Gardner, Mrs. Emma Gensel,

Mrs. Annie Glanding, Mrs. Maria Goodall, Miss Mary Gowen, Miss Ida B. Graham, Bates J. Griswold.

Miss Fannie Habich, Mrs. Jane Haff, Miss Ella Hall, Mrs. Phoebe Hamilton, Thomas Harkness, Mrs. S. Harper, William B. Hens, Miss Ella Hook, Miss Lizzie Hulse, Charles Hunter, Mrs. Kate Hunter.

Miss Lulu Jardine, Miss Mary Jones, Miss Annie Keller, Samuel M. Kennedy, Mrs. Jane Kennedy, Miss Mary Kennedy, Miss Annie Kennedy, Mrs. Jennie Kennedy, William P. Kirby, Christian Kleinhenn, Miss Martha Klenneck, Charles Kruse, John Kugler, Mrs. C. Kugler, Mrs. Kate Kugler.

Mrs. C. Langman, Mrs. R. Leighton, James Leo, Charles Lesley, Mrs. K. E. Lesley, Frank Lesley, Miss Kate Linsenmeyer, Thomas Little, Mrs. Lizzie Little, Theodore H. Loder, Mrs. E. H. Loder.

Miss Jennie Magee, Andrew Martin, Mrs. Ida Martin, John Martin, Mrs. Sallie Martin, William Matlack, Mrs. Mary E. McAninch, Ira B. McCormick, Mrs. Maggie McCormick, Mrs. Elizabeth McCoy, Mrs. Susan McFarland, Miss Bella McIntire, Miss Bella McKeever, Miss Agnes McNevin, Mrs. Margaret Meares, Miss Priscilla Meloy, Miss Lottie Milden, Mrs. Louise E. Miller, Mrs. Mary V. Mitchell, Fred Mohr, Miss Martha Morrow, Miss Lizzie A. Murray.

Miss Cora Narrigan, Mrs. Adele Nifenecker, Miss Camille Nifenecker, Alexander Nixon, Mrs. Eliza Nixon, Miss Mary Nixon, Miss Martha Nixon.

William W. O'Brien, Robert C. Ogden, Mrs. Ellen Ogden, Miss Julia T. Ogden, Charles A. Oliver, Miss Katie O'Neil, Miss Lizzie Orr, Mr. and Mrs. David Orr.

Miss Mary Parvin, Miss Ridie L. Parvin, Miss Kate Parvin, Mrs. Lizzie Pessano, Miss E. L. Pinkerton, Miss Lillie Poole, Mrs. Beulah Powell, Victor Powers.

James Radcliffe, Mrs. Charlotte Ramsay, Mrs. A. Randolph, William P. Rawlings, James Reid, Mrs. Rebecca Reid, Mrs. Margaret Reilly, D. R. Reynolds, W. R. Reynolds, W. W. Reynolds, D. C. Reynolds, M.D., Mrs. D. C. Reynolds, George C. Reynolds, Miss Laura Rhoades, Mrs. Margaret Rhoades, Mrs. R. Richards, Mrs. Kate Robinson, Mrs. Jane Russell, Robert Russell.

Mrs. S. A. Scofield, Mrs. Elizabeth Semple, Mrs. Sadie Siemen, Miss Sallie Shingle, Miss Nellie R. Smith, Mrs. Mary Smith, Mrs. Clara Smith, Daniel R. Smith, Mrs. A. Steele, George W. Steinbach, Mrs. Margaret Steinbach, Joseph Sterrett, Mrs. Mary Sterrett, A. A. Stevenson, John W. Stewart, Mrs. Jane S. Stewart, Mrs. Margaret Stewart, Miss Mary C. Stewart, Miss Martha B. Stewart.

Mrs. Mary Tafford, Benjamin Tafford, James C. Taylor, Mrs. Kate Taylor, Miss Jeannie L. Thompson, Miss W. Trautvetter, Miss Annie Trautvetter.

Miss Katie Vance, Mrs. Mary Voudersmith, Miss Mary B. Vondersmith.

Miss Minnie Wagner, Samuel Walker, Mrs. S. J. Walker, Samuel O. Walker, Miss Lucy Walker, Mrs. Anna Ware, Mrs Emma Warren, Mrs. Ann J. Waters, Miss Mary Waters, Mrs. H. H. Watt, Mrs. H. Webb, J. M. Weiss, Mrs. Anna Weiss, Mrs. Eliza White, Miss Stella White, Mrs. Sarah Wiley, Robert Williamson, Mrs. Sarah Williamson, Miss Della Wilson.

Mrs. Sophie Young, Mrs. Fanny Young.

Dr. Miller was installed as the first pastor on the 23rd of April, 1882. At the May meeting of the General Assembly of that year, the church reported a membership of 259, and a Sunday-school membership of 1024.

The *Hollond Monthly*, of February, 1883, had this to say of Dr. Miller's second anniversary: "It was a time of thanksgiving, for his work has been signally blessed of God. Not only are we organized into a church, bound more closely together by the bands of love and sympathy, and to the Saviour by increased devotion, but also our number has been augmented by the addition of 169 precious souls won for Jesus."

On the 3rd of September, 1883, the pastoral relation existing between Dr. Miller and the church was dissolved, Dr. Miller resigning in order that he might give his time more fully to the duties connected with his position in the editorial department of the Board of Publication and Sabbath-school Work, a position he had held before and during his pastoral care over Hollond.   His resignation was regretfully accepted.

The Rev. William M. Paden, who had graduated from the Princeton Theological Seminary in the spring, accepted the call extended to him by the church to become its pastor, and with consecrated enthusiasm entered upon the work October 7th, 1883.   He was ordained and installed on the 20th of the following November.   The sermon was delivered by the Rev. John S. MacIntosh, D.D., the charge to the pastor by the Rev. William Brenton Greene, D.D., and the charge to the people by the Rev. Dr. Miller.

When Mr. Paden was away the next year, on his first vacation, Dr. Miller wrote the following words of commendation in the *Hollond Monthly* : " Mr. Paden has won the love of all hearts.   He has become a welcome visitor in all the people's homes.   His words in the pulpit are listened to with eagerness, and many are helped and strengthened by them.   His

ministrations in the households where sickness
and sorrow have called him, have been tender
and consoling. His words spoken by the way,
have been wise and faithful. It would be hard
to find a church anywhere more proud of its
pastor than Hollond.''

Mr. Paden continued to work with marked
ability and success, but as the field enlarged
and the outlook grew more and more encouraging, it was felt that no one man could hope
to meet successfully the demands which such a
task would impose upon his time and strength,
so Dr. Miller was cordially invited to assist Mr.
Paden in the work.   Under the title, '' A
Happy Combination,'' the *Hollond Monthly*, of
January, 1886, thus speaks of this forward
movement :

'' The heavy pressure of parish work, added
to the preparations for pulpit duties, have laid
a heavy burden upon Mr. Paden. Not but
that he could and would carry it, but the cares
have become so exacting as to keep him almost
entirely from that quiet and deliberate study
which, as a young minister, he deems essential
to proper growth. This has been a matter of
conference between him and friends, both
within and without our church.

'' It is but natural that under these circumstances, the plan of inviting Rev. Dr. Miller
to associate himself in the pastoral office with

REV. WILLIAM M. PADEN, D. D.

Mr. Paden should suggest itself to several minds simultaneously. The peculiarly happy relations existing between the church and both its pastors, and the continuance of Dr. Miller in the active work of the church and school since he retired from the pastorate, added to the close personal relations existing between the two men, give testimony at once to the propriety and success of such a plan, could it be adopted.

" Upon investigation, it has been found in every way feasible, and, by the action of the session and trustees upon the one part, and Dr. Miller upon the other, an arrangement has been made whereby he will become immediately Mr. Paden's associate in the pastorate of the church. The whole arrangement is pervaded by so deep a cordiality, and is evidently so much in harmony with a spirit of earnest Christian work, that it promises great things for the work in Hollond."

And so, indeed, it proved. Through the consecrated and untiring efforts of these devoted men, blessed by God, an era of prosperity was entered upon which soon made the work an important centre of Christian usefulness.

The church, after its organization in 1882, held its services, thanks to the Tenth Church, in the chapel, which, however well adapted to Sunday-school work, was unsuited to the needs of a growing congregation. It soon became evident that a new church building was necessary, and plans were at once instituted to raise money for that purpose. As early as November of the same year, the following announcement appeared in the *Hollond Monthly:* "Our 'Brick Fund,' which is the Sunday-school work for the future church building, now amounts to $898.76."

The next month a "Children's Parlor Fair" was held by Miss Helen Ogden, and in April, 1883, a "Japanese Tea Party" was given. At the business meeting of the congregation on the 21st of January, 1884, Mr. William L. Cooke, the treasurer, announced "a balance on hand of above $1,200 belonging to the Church Building Fund, the result of the 'Brick Books,' the 'Children's Parlor Fair,' held by one of the scholars at her home, and the 'Japanese Tea Party.' Little Margaretta Morris' two dollars, given at Christmas, has been made a nest egg for 'The Hollond,' as that was the object to which she in love gave it."

Miss Ogden afterwards became one of our most efficient teachers. As the wife of Mr. Alexander Purves, also a former Hollond teacher and now treasurer of the Hampton Institute, Virginia, she is in a position to render much valuable service to the great educational institution of which her father, Mr. Robert C. Ogden, is the president. The "little Margaretta Morris" referred to is now a beloved teacher in our school. She was the only child of Mr. Charles E. Morris, and it is with special pride and pleasure that we find her giving much of her time to the work to which her father was so devotedly attached, and in which her mother has been so long and so helpfully engaged as a teacher.

On Sunday, June 15th, 1884, the importance of a new building was brought directly to the attention of the people, and in the giving that followed there were many touching evidences of the devotion of all to the work. Through subscriptions received that day from the church and the school, the fund was increased to $7,178.21. This sum, with $5,000 from the estate of the late Rev. Henry A. Boardman,

D.D., was sufficient to pay for the land, with quite a little sum left over for the building. Soon after, the lot on the south-east corner of Broad and Federal streets was purchased—Mr. Amos Dotterer, a trustee, advancing $3,600, Mr. W. L. Cooke $1,400 and Miss L. S. Penrose $1,000, until the subscriptions should be paid in. These subscriptions were nearly all paid before the close of the year.

The purchase of the lot was an important forward movement, and greatly increased the interest of the congregation in the work. The fund continued to grow. A "Garden Party" at Mr. William L. Cooke's was highly successful; the Mite Society, of which Miss Lydia S. Penrose was the president, was organized about this time and was of material help; a contribution was received through Mr. James Whyte, a valued teacher, from the Sunday-school of Ayr, Scotland; Chinamen in San Rafael, California, "out of their poverty found something to send as a kindly response to a gift previously sent to them from Hollond;" the Ansonia Clock Company and the New Haven Clock Company sent contributions through Benjamin J. Cooke, a scholar in Professor Edward MacHarg's class; members of the Tenth Church made liberal subscriptions; many friends manifested their interest by substantial donations; and, best of all, the people themselves, by far the larger number being poor or in moderate circumstances, made splendid sacrifices in order that the needed funds might be obtained.

We have spoken only of some of the *beginnings;* it would be difficult to mention all the sources through which assistance came at various times. To those familiar with these anxious days of preparation it seems as if human love and self-denial were intertwined with every stone and added to the sacredness of every portion of the beautiful structure which has since been erected to the glory of God and for the advancement of his kingdom here among men. It was almost a literal reproduction of the golden time of Isaiah when, "They helped every one his neighbor; and every one said to his brother, ' Be of good courage! ' " Brave-hearted boys and girls, striving to make meager salaries meet life's necessities, denied themselves that the work might go on; toil-worn men and women, struggling with the grave problems of existence, forgot themselves and their needs in their devotion to the general good; followers of many creeds, with disinterested generosity, helped to make the burdens lighter; and natives of many lands, by their practical sympathy and aid, attested the brotherhood of man. Is it any wonder, then, that we now glory in the freedom of our pews, and welcome all visitors, without regard to race, creed, or social condition, to share with us in the privilege of worshipping God in our temple beautiful !

Among the friends of the church who gave $250.00 and over to the Building Fund and whose names do not appear on our list of members, are the following: Mrs. Gustavus Benson, $500.00; Col. R. Dale Benson, $500.00; John S. Bispham, $250.00; John H. Converse, $500.00; Robert Creswell, $500.00; Miss Creswell, $300.00; A. Boyd Cummings, $5,000.00; Thomas Dolan, $500.00; William L. DuBois, $1,000.00; W.W. Frazier, $500.00; Mrs. Louis R. Fox, $1,000.00; B. W. Greer, $500.00; George Griffiths, $500.00; Mrs. Charles E. Morris, $4,000 ; Jonathan Ogden, $500.00 ; Mrs. Slaymaker, $500.00; Estate of Miss Margaret Smith, $500.00; James Spear, $500.00; Charles N. Thorpe, $500.00; R. S. Walton, $650.00 ; Thomas B. Wanamaker, $2,500 ; John Wanamaker, $5,000.00.

In his ninth anniversary sermon, delivered in the chapel on Sunday morning, October 2d, 1892, Dr. Paden thus spoke of some of the early plans for the new building:

" My best conceptions of the mission of this church have come out of the development of the church itself. When I came here nine years ago, I had no overmastering desire to

enter upon the work of building a new church.
I thought the chapel quite equal to the field;
when I found out better, my first thought was
to compromise with the Lord, and advocate
the building of a little church against the
chapel. It would cost less and save time,
said Prudence. But the Lord checkmated
that scheme by refusing to interfere with the
blacksmith shop on an adjoining lot. He
probably knew that it was a better place for a
blacksmith shop than for a church. Then we
said: It's expensive—too expensive; but perhaps we would better buy the Broad street
property; there is nothing to hinder us from
building an inexpensive church, even if we are
obliged to build it on a costly lot. We set out
to build a thirty-thousand dollar church. We
soon found, however, that we could not build
a church that would suit the field, even on
paper, for thirty thousand dollars. We screwed
our courage up to the thought of raising forty
thousand dollars; and a committee was asked
to look about for a church to suit the field and
our faith. Meanwhile, our ideas were expand-
ing, our hearts enlarging, and the resources
and responsibilities of the young church becoming more evident. As one of the conse-
quences, the committee came back with some
of the disillusionment a mother experiences
when she goes to the store one of these autumn

days with her strapping fifteen-year-old boy. She takes money to pay for a boy's suit, and finds out that nothing will suit him but men's styles and sizes. So our committee came back, saying: We cannot build a church of the size and sort we need for the Hollond force and field for forty or fifty thousand dollars. They thought it might be done for sixty-five or seventy thousand, without trimmings; but, what was more to the point, they were ready, and they found the trustees ready, and the trustees found you ready, to undertake the building of the best church we could plan for the force and the field, whatever the cost. In all this I believe the Lord has directed our steps. He has directed us in our delays. He has directed us in the development of our ideas; and if we have done wrong in going beyond the forty-thousand dollar limit, the Lord has already given us double for all such sins. He has given us eighty thousand dollars, and we have every sign of his continued favor.''

The trustees, under the inspiring leadership of Mr. Ogden, and helped and encouraged always by the pastors, gave the most painstaking and unwavering oversight to the many serious and perplexing problems which so constantly confronted them at this period. With a faithfulness worthy of the highest commen-

dation, and with a devotion which should
never be forgotten, they sought to the utmost
of their ability to secure the plans of a building which would combine beauty and comfort
with churchly dignity and durability, and
which would be in every way worthy of the
commanding position it was to occupy.   In
this, as events proved, they were signally
successful.

THE NEW BUILDING

The ground for the new building was broken by Mr. William L. Cooke, chairman of the building committee, at 5 o'clock Wednesday afternoon, October 23, 1889. Drs. Paden and Miller, Dr. William Brenton Greene, Jr., pastor of the old Tenth Church, and Mr. Robert C. Ogden, also took an active part in the service. Soon after, the cellar was dug and the heavy foundation walls placed in position.

On Saturday afternoon, May 31, 1890, the corner-stone was laid by Dr. J. R. Miller, with impressive ceremonies, in the **CORNER-STONE LAYING** presence of a large gathering of happy people. Dr. Paden made a brief address of welcome, Dr. William Hutton offered a prayer, Dr. J. C. Thompson read the scriptures (1. Peter, 2 : 1–9), Mr. Robert C. Ogden made a "statement of progress," Dr. William Brenton Greene, Jr., delivered an address, Dr. Paden announced the contents of the box to be placed in the corner-stone, the stone was laid by Dr. Miller with prayer,

HOLLOND MEMORIAL CHURCH

Dr. Charles A. Dickey made an address, and Dr. Willard M. Rice pronounced the benediction.

The following articles were placed in the box :

Bible; Confession of Faith and Shorter Catechism; Book of Worship of Hollond Sunday-school; programme of the ground-breaking of the building; Memorial of Charles E. Morris; short history of the church ; programme of the laying of the corner-stone; Westminster Teacher; "In His Steps," by Dr. Miller ; bronze medal of the Centennial General Assembly; medal of the Centenary of Presbyterianism in the United States; rules of the Ministering Ten and of the King's Daughters, with the talent envelope used by Dr. Miller's Sunday-school class in collecting for the building fund; description of work at Hollond, by Dr. W. M. Paden, as given at the Buffalo Convention; roll of officers and teachers of the Sunday-school; constitution and roll of officers of Young People's Association; roll of officers of missionary societies; roll of officers of the church; prayer-meeting topic card; brick book collection envelope; American flag; postal card and stamps; *Presbyterian Journal; The Presbyterian;* New York *Observer; Sunday School Times; The Independent*, four copies, containing a full discussion of the Revision question;

morning and afternoon papers, and the *Ledger* almanac.

Dr. Paden, in concluding the reading of the list, said, "Many of these are small things, but as the mark of the bird's wing in the sand-stone has made history so may some of these little things."

At a meeting of the congregation held on Monday evening, February 13, 1893, to pass upon the series of resolutions presented for consideration **FREE PEWS** relative to the system to be adopted in reference to sittings in the new church when it should be completed, it was heartily and unanimously resolved that all the seats should be *absolutely free and unassigned*. This had been the policy of the church from its organization.

The following article, from the pen of Dr. Miller, appeared in the *New York Evangelist*, on the 23d of the same month. It admirably presents the case in all its bearings :

"The subject of 'free pews' has excited considerable interest in this city as well as elsewhere during the past year. Reference has already been made in this correspondence to the Hollond Memorial Church, as being thoroughly committed to this plan of support and benevolence. During the twelve years of its history it has worked along this line with constantly improving results and with growing satisfaction among its people.

" Mr. Robert C. Ogden has been identified with this church from the beginning as superintendent of the Sabbath-school, elder, and president of the board of trustees. Mr. Ogden's views on the subject of 'free pews' are well known, especially through his admirable address on the subject a year ago, which was published by the Fleming H. Revell Company, and has had a wide sale.

" The Hollond Church system is not only no pew rents, but no pledges of any sort. Envelopes are used, and each member contributes each Lord's day, as the Lord has prospered him and his own conscience dictates, he and the treasurer alone knowing how much he gives.

" The new church building of this congregation is approaching completion, and the question has been under consideration, whether the pews shall be assigned to families and others, by lot or otherwise, or whether no assignment whatever shall be made. The subject has had patient and careful thought, and has been much discussed among the people. The decision has been reached that no assignment of any pews or sittings shall be made. The whole house will be free—as free to the stranger coming in any Sunday as to the member who has been longest in connection with the church.

"This is practically a new departure, at least for Philadelphia; indeed, it is doubtful whether any Presbyterian church in the country has tried the experiment, and its working will be attentively watched by many people. The decision of the church on the matter at the congregational meeting held on the 13th inst. was unanimously made. The people themselves settled it without any urging or persuading by any advocate whatever. The feeling is that any assignment of pews, however qualified, would be an encroachment on the absolute freeness of the church, which must be maintained as a cardinal principle of its organization and system. As a matter of fact, there is no doubt that most of the families and members will practically settle down in a little while into certain pews, where they will habitually sit. But as there has been no assignment of the pews, no one can assert a claim to any sitting, however long he may have occupied it. No person coming into the church at any time and having been shown into a pew, need fear that he is in any other person's place, for nobody will have a place which is his own. Respect will, of course, be paid by regular worshippers to the preferences and habits of fellow-worshippers. The ushers, too, will regard the desires of families and individuals as far as pos-

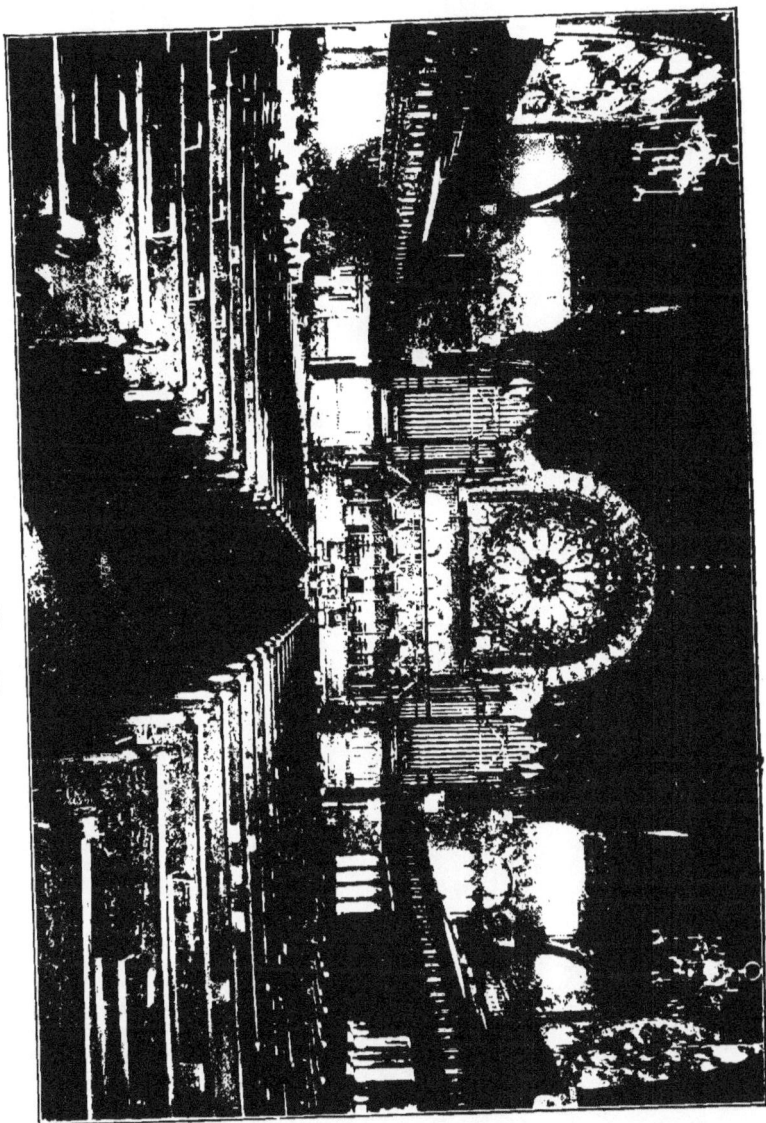

EAST ROSE WINDOW

sible, not putting strangers into pews which
they know to be ordinarily occupied by members, unless it be necessary to do so.   Then it
is to be hoped that the spirit of hospitality will
be so thoroughly developed and so practically
dominant that they will think always of others,
not of themselves, taking the place of hosts in
the house of God, not of guests, and giving to
any one who enters the door a true welcome in
the name of the Lord.   For, after all, whatever
the method of church support, and whatever
the manner of distributing the worshippers in
the pews, the members of the church are responsible for the character of the welcome
given to strangers.   In a free pew, as well as
in one rented at the highest price, an occupant
can freeze a visitor by a look, if the inhospit-
able spirit be in his heart.   The only way to
make a church with free pews and unassigned
sittings, or any other church, a place where
anybody will feel at home, is to have the spirit
of love, the mind of Christ, ruling among the
people.''

Many causes combined to prevent the completion of the building at as early a date as had
been anticipated, and the trustees
were often compelled to have re-
DEDICATION course to '' wise and masterly inactivity.''   The work, however,
though slow at times and often delayed, was

done thoroughly. At length, to the great joy of all, there came

"A day in golden letters to be set
Among the high tides of the calendar,"

when the hopes of the building committee were to have glad fruition and the patience of the congregation was to be richly rewarded—the eventful day of occupancy, *Monday, October 16, 1893!*

On Sunday, October 15, the last preaching services were held in the chapel. Heaven never gave to earth a more beautiful day. The room was crowded. In the morning Dr. Miller preached from the texts: "*Remember the words of the Lord Jesus, how he said, It is more blessed to give than to receive.* Acts 20: 35; "*Remember the word unto thy servant, upon which thou hast caused me to hope.*" Ps. 119: 49.

In speaking of those who once were with us, he said: "They labored, suffered and died before they saw the finished work. They did their part, and passed to their reward; the work has fallen to us. Their hands are folded now, but we must not fold our hands until *our* work is done."

In the evening Dr. Paden preached from Ezekiel 3: 12, "*I heard behind me a voice of a great rushing, saying, Blessed be the glory of the Lord from his place.*" The sermon was largely made up of readings from reminiscent letters written by those who had long labored for the church. The benediction was pronounced at five minutes of nine o'clock, and at 9.23 the last lingering worshipper had departed, the lights were extinguished, and the building was left alone with its memories. It continues to be used for Sabbath-school and prayer-meeting purposes.

On the next evening, Monday, October 16th, the dedicatory services, which were delightfully helpful and interesting, commenced in the new church and continued throughout the week. At his own request, the beautiful plants with which the building was decorated were contributed by a member of the Roman Catholic Church. The pulpit Bible also was presented by a friend of the Roman Catholic Church "as a mark of his appreciation of the kindness members of Hollond had shown to him and his family." The communion table was a gift from Mr. John D. McCord.

The first sermon was by Dr. Miller, and his text was from Heb. 13: 8, "*Jesus Christ the same yesterday, and to-day, and for ever.*" "That name," said Dr. Miller, "is far above all others for salvation, for help, for comfort, for refuge. In the hour of temptation it is a name of strength ; in the hour of trouble, of need, of pain, it is a name of hope.

Compared to it all other names fade as the stars before the sun. Christ in his person is always the same. Before his incarnation, as now, he felt the same ardent love for sinners on earth. He is the same to the world ; no man spake as this man ; His words are eternal. He is the same ; unchangeable ; in redemption the light of the cross shines down through all ages. Men may come and go, but Jesus Christ is the same yesterday, to-day and forever.''

Addresses were made by ex-Mayor Edwin S. Stuart and Mr. R. C. Ogden. Tuesday evening was devoted to the interests of the Christian Endeavor Society. Addresses were made by Dr. William M. Paden, G. S. Benson, Esq., and the Rev. J. T. Beckley, D. D., pastor of the Beth-Eden Baptist Church. Mr. Charles A. Hoehling was installed as president of the Christian Endeavor Society. Wednesday evening, there were greetings by the Rev. Thomas A. Hoyt, D. D., pastor of Chambers Presbyterian Church, and a sermon by the Rev. John R. Paxton, D. D., of New York. The sermon on Thursday evening, was by the Rev. Dr. Charles Cuthbert Hall, of Brooklyn. Mr. Leonard E. Auty, the famous tenor soloist, sang. The benediction was pronounced by Dr. W. C. Cattell. Addresses were made on Friday evening by the Rev. James D. Paxton, of the West Spruce

NORTH ROSE WINDOW

Street Presbyterian Church, Rev. H. L. Duhring, of the Episcopal Church, and the Rev. S. W. Dana, D. D., of the Walnut Street Presbyterian Church. Mr. Murray Chism and his sister sang duets. The church was filled to overflowing at every service. The weather during the entire week was delightful.

The dedicatory sermon was preached on Sunday morning October 22d, by the Rev. Dr. Paden, from the text : " *Therefore let no man glory in men. For all things are yours ; whether Paul, or Apollos, or Cephas, or the world, or life, or death, or things present, or things to come ; all are yours ; and ye are Christ's ; and Christ is God's.*" 1 Cor. 3 : 21-23. Among other things he said : " Partisanship is carnality, not piety." " When will we learn that there is nothing essentially pious either in swearing by or swearing at Luther or Loyola, Calvin or Wesley, Spurgeon or Newman, or Martineau ? Christianity is not loyalty to human leadership, but loyalty to Christ." " Thomas a Kempis, Bunyan, Rutherford and Woolman, do not belong to the Catholics, Baptists, Presbyterians or Quakers ; they belong to us all. All things are yours." " This is not the church of St. John, or St. Paul, or St. David, much less of St. Calvin, or St. Wesley ; it is the church of Christ."

" A Protestant church? Yes; but Christian first, Protestant second. A Presbyterian church? Yes; but Christian first, Protestant second, and Presbyterian with what is left over." "We have at one communion received members by letters from seven different denominations. Our enlistments by confession come from homes of almost every denominational congregation. We receive all alike on the one condition: ' Faith in the Lord Jesus Christ, manifest in Godly sorrow for sin, and in a Godly life.' Our question is not, Are you a Paulite, or a Methodist, or a Presbyterian, or a Baptist; but, Do you want to fall in with us in our following of Jesus Christ? You can no more keep a man out of Christ's Church, for the cut of his theology, than you can for the cut of his coat."

" The Christian Church must be as broad as Christendom. Christian character must be as broad as life."

At 2.30 in the afternoon, 1300 out of 1500 scholars marched from the chapel into the new church. After the doxology, the first hymn sung was, "Come, Thou Almighty King." Addresses were made by Dr. Willard M. Rice, R. S. Walton, Esq., and the Hon. George S. Graham. Mr. Walton's helpful talk was on, " Mind the steps," his three stepping stones being, "*Be true ; be trusty ; be noble.*"

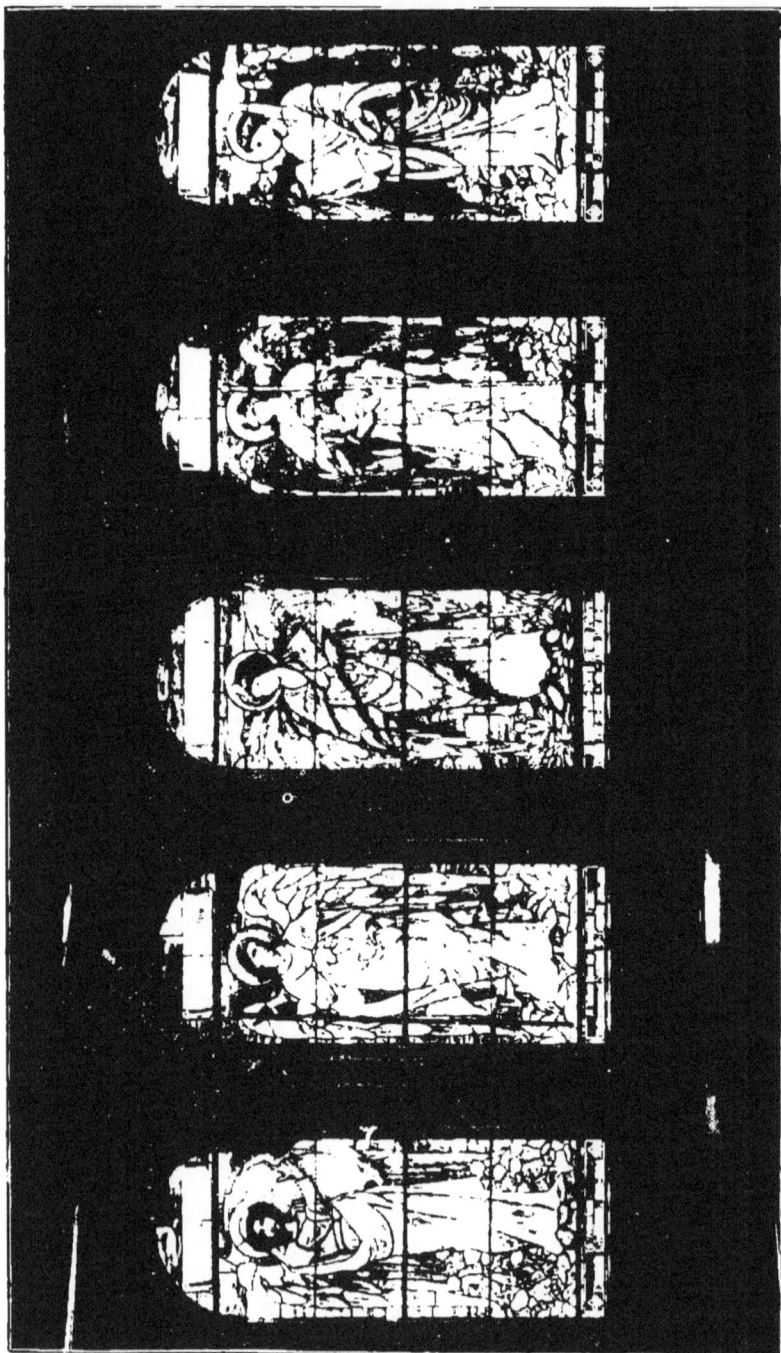

The closing services of the dedication were held in the evening, Dr. Miller presiding. The keys were delivered to Mr. Robert C. Ogden, chairman of the trustees, by Mr. Wm L. Cooke, chairman of the building committee. Addresses were made by the Rev. Louis R. Fox and the Hon. John Wanamaker. Madame Suelke sang, and a congratulatory letter was read from the Rev. Wm. Brenton Greene, Jr., D. D., who was unable to be present.

The day, which had been cloudy, ended with a down-pour of rain. The church, however, was filled to its utmost capacity.

Mr. William L. Cooke wears on his watch chain a highly-prized gold dollar which was presented to him during dedication week by Dr. Paden. This dollar was given to Dr. Paden on the day the ground for the new building was broken and is marked with that date—" Hollond Memorial, October 23d, 1889."

The new church is of noble proportions, and is without doubt, the most imposing structure of its kind in South Philadelphia. THE NEW BUILDING The outer walls, which have a frontage on Broad street of ninety-four feet and a depth of one hundred and nine feet on Federal street, are constructed of Ohio buff Massilon stone, with trimmings of red sand-stone from the

L. cf C.

famous Ballochmyle quarries of Scotland, the
two colors most happily blending. The two
entrances on Broad street are through vestibules sixteen feet square, lighted by handsome
memorial windows. There is also an entrance,
through a vestibule, on Federal street. The
roof, which is covered with Roman tiling of
a bright rich color, forms a most harmonious
contrast with the walls and is strikingly attractive.

A massive stone tower, 150 feet in height,
adds greatly to the artistic appearance of the
building, and is one of the most conspicuous
land-marks on South Broad street. The
church is cruciform in shape, and of the Ro-
manesque order of architecture. In its interior
construction the architect, Mr. David S. Gen-
dell (assisted by Mr. Thomas Jamieson as
supervising architect) while yielding to the
modern demand for a square amphitheatre,
happily retained all the desirable features of
an ecclesiastical building, many of which are
so conspicuously lacking in the churches of the
present day.

The heavy oaken pews, beautifully uphol-
stered, are arranged in semi-circular form, and
give the church a seating capacity of 1,200.
The inner roof is of the open timber construction, and is finished in oak, as are all of the
interior decorations. Even the smallest details

of the work bear evidence of beauty, strength, and durability. The building is heated by steam and lighted by both gas and electricity —the latter was used for the first time on Sunday evening, July 31st, 1898. The fixtures were made by Cornelius & Rowland from specially prepared designs. A comfortable, well-appointed study is at the left of the pulpit.

The following appeared in the *Presbyterian Observer* of February 7th, 1895 : "One of the best and latest works of modern architects is the Hollond Memorial Church. For harmonious proportions, intricately carved woodwork, rich and suggestive stained glass windows and appropriate furnishings, this building is not surpassed, and, so far as I know, is unequaled in Philadelphia."

The most earnest and painstaking attention was given by the trustees to the windows, which represent the supreme efforts of the best stained-glass artists of Philadelphia and New York. Tiffany, Armstrong, and Godwin have here their finest conceptions crystalized in stone and glass. On every side are figures of saints and apostles, angels and arch-angels, produced in all the marvellous combinations of coloring which have made the works of the old masters the wonder

THE WINDOWS

of succeeding ages. The worshipper whose
heart is open to the touch of the beautiful here
gets soul-ennobling sermons other than those
preached from the sacred desk, and he receives benedictions as divine as those from the
lips of the pastors. Hopeless, indeed, must be
the lot of him who heedless of the teachings
of Christ through his ministers, also feels no
longings for better things when God speaks to
his innermost being through these matchless
creations of art.

In each of the four gables of the church is a
large rose window, twenty-one feet in diameter.
Perhaps the most beautiful of
these is the one in the east gable,
directly back of the pulpit. It
is a masterpiece of decorative art,
and cannot fail to excite the admiration of all
beholders. Over the little oriental town of
Bethlehem in the center shines out clear and
bright the Star of the Nativity ; and although
we cannot see the manger, nor hear the singing, we instinctively feel, with Dr. J. G. Holland, that

THE EAST ROSE WINDOW

> There's a song in the air !
> There's a star in the sky !
> There's a mother's deep prayer
> And a baby's low cry ;
> And the star rains its fire while the beautiful
>   sing,
> For the manger of Bethlehem cradles a king !

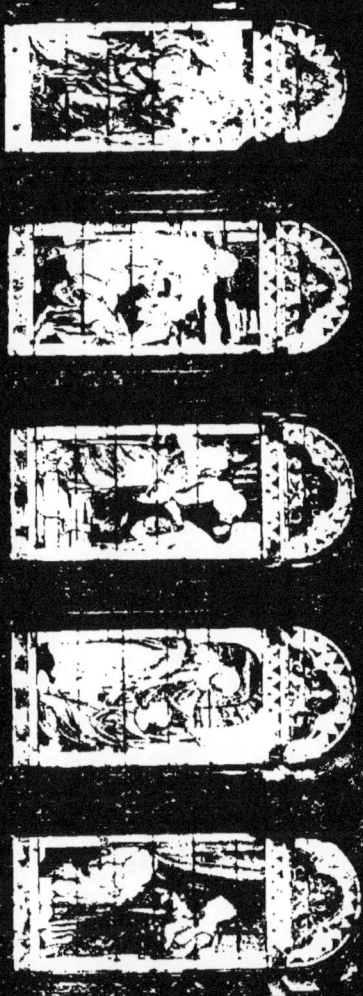

There's a tumult of joy
O'er the wonderful birth,
For the Virgin's sweet boy
Is the Lord of the earth.
Ay, the star rains its fire, and the beautiful sing,
For the manger of Bethlehem cradles a king!

In the light of that star
Lie the ages impearled ;
And that song from afar
Has swept over the world :
Every heart is aflame, and the beautiful sing,
In the homes of the nations, that Jesus is king!

We rejoice in the light,
And we echo the song
That comes down through the night
From the heavenly throng.
Ay, we shout to the lovely evangel they bring,
And we greet in his cradle our Saviour and
King!

In four of the sixteen segments which radiate from the center, are flame colors that represent, or rather suggest, the Cross, and in the intermediate segments are groups of happy cherubs flying toward the town. There are thirty-six of these beautiful figures, and they are so naturally and gracefully arranged as to relieve the work of all suggestion of stiffness. A wrapt expression of holy joy and adoration is on each face, and, as we look, our thoughts turn reverently to the deathless night of long ago when o'er the Judean plains was heard "the heavenly host praising God and saying, 'Glory to God in the highest, and on earth peace, good will toward men.'" The artist has happily caught the inspiration of the hour and through his masterful skill the song still trembles on the air and falls as a benediction on all hearts that worship the Father in spirit and in truth in this his earthly temple.

Though immediately back of the pulpit the coloring is so skillfully modified that even in the brightest morning light the speaker is never thrown into shadow. The window was made by Alfred Godwin, after designs of Frederick Wilson. It is a memorial from the women of the church to Charles E. Morris, "whose faithful service and inspiring leadership in the past history of Hollond made the new church possible."

The rose window in the west gable was designed and executed by Maitland Armstrong, a master of color in glass. In view of the intricate stone tracery, which is altogether different from that of the east window, it was necessary to follow purely decorative designs, with no attempt at illustration. The many colors, in which the pale warm reds predominate, are artistically blended. The glow of the afternoon sunlight is needed to display its beauty to the best advantage.

THE WEST ROSE WINDOW

In this window an interesting effort has been made to illustrate the "fruits of the Holy Spirit." The central figure rep-

THE NORTH ROSE WINDOW resents the ascending Christ, with hands raised in benediction. Immediately above, is the descending dove, indicating the coming of the Holy Spirit after the departure of Christ from the earth, as foretold in the fourteenth chapter of St. John. Angel ministrants surround the ascending Lord, while in the larger circles beyond, the fruits of the Spirit—"Love, Joy, Peace, Longsuffering, Gentleness, Goodness, Faith, Meekness, and Temperance," (Galatians, 5 : 22, 23)—are represented by figures of mortals. It was a brilliant conception which thus so successfully blended the divine, the angelic, and the human in this very intimate but distinct relationship. This window also was made by Alfred Godwin from drawing by Frederick Wilson. It is a memorial to a sister of Mr. Robert C. Ogden, Mrs. Helen Ogden Wood.

The stone tracery of this window is exactly similar in design to the one in the north gable.

THE SOUTH ROSE WINDOW At present it is filled with plain glass painted to harmonize with its general setting. This painting has been done so well as to make a surprisingly good appearance. It is hoped that this glass will, at no distant day, be removed and its place taken by a handsome memorial.

Under each of the four rose windows is a group of five arcade windows. Those in the north, south, and west walls are **THE EAST ARCADE WINDOWS** about three feet wide and eight feet high. The windows in the east wall are somewhat smaller. This difference was made necessary by the location and design of the choir, which is between them and the pulpit. From the floor of the choir to the base line of the arcade windows the wall is covered by an oak wainscoting, and the diminution of the windows was compelled by this decoration, and by the necessity of keeping all exterior light above the pulpit and choir. The design used in these windows is, in the main, merely a decorative, geometrical pattern, and is alike in all, slight variations in the color of the several windows giving moderate contrasts. In the arch at the top of each window is a cherub's head, serving to associate the thought of the music below with that of the heavenly host represented in the great rose window just above.

These windows complete the memorial to Charles E. Morris, of which the east rose window is, of course, the important part. Alfred Godwin was the maker.

Under the north gallery is a group of five

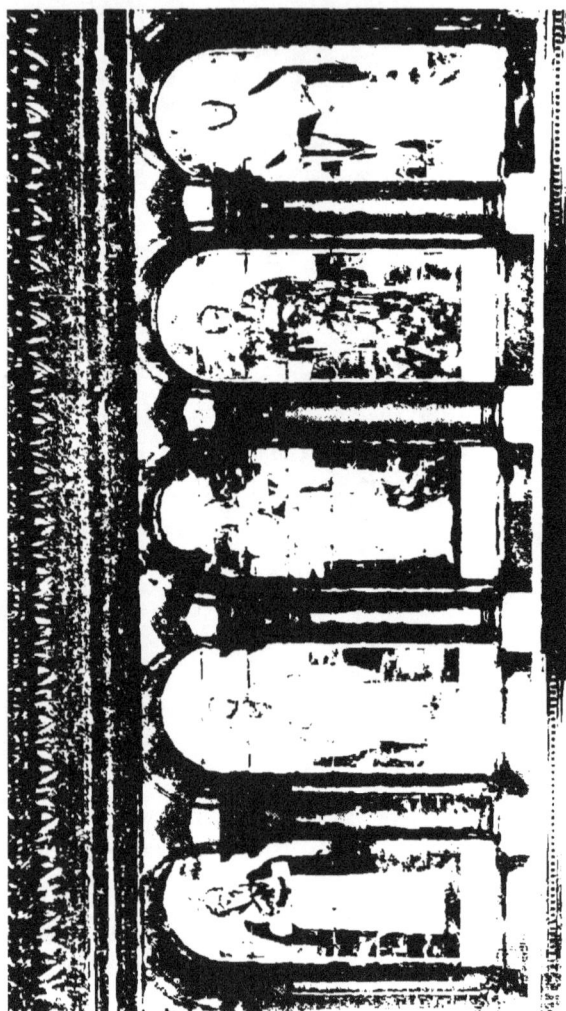

attractive windows. The figures, while not
original in design, are of such
THE exquisite workmanship as to
NORTH ARCADE make one quite indifferent to
WINDOWS the fact that they are copies
—especially is this true when we learn that
they were made from models, designed by the
master hand of Sir Edward Burne-Jones, now
in important English churches—the central one
being from a church in Brighton, and the
others from Salisbury Cathedral. The windows are of a highly decorative character, and
are all idealized angelic figures of the type for
which Sir Edward is distinguished. The rich
and harmonious coloring was the work of
Alfred Godwin, who followed the originals in
design but adapted the color scheme to the
location of the windows and to the general
light of the church.

These windows are all memorials. The first
on the left is to the memory of Elizabeth C.
Williams (1860-1884) ; the second was presented by the Thoughtful Circle of King's
Daughters to the memory of Samuel M.
Kennedy (1853-1893); the third was given
by Miss Penrose's Sunday-school class to the
memory of Dr. Paden's brother, Henry Armine
Paden (1857-1892); and the fourth and fifth
are memorials of Alice Slaymaker (1867-1896),
and Bertha M. Slaymaker (1864–1877).

A pathetic interest attaches to the Slaymaker sisters. They were not connected with Hollond. Dr. Miller was the friend of one of these (Alice), and he visited her frequently during her long illness. She was a great sufferer but the peace of her heart was never shadowed. Her sister also lived a joyous Christian life, brief though it was. When both had gone home, there were some precious savings which were to be devoted to whatever sacred use the parents might designate. They were given to the new Hollond building, and being put at interest, the sum grew to five hundred dollars—the cost of the two memorials.

The five arcade windows in the west wall were the gift of the King's Daughters, and are no less beautiful illustrations of THE WEST ARCADE WINDOWS the loving ministry of the donors than they are of the perfection which may be attained in the art which gave them being. They vividly depict the different scenes described in Matthew 25: 35, 36: (1) "I was an hungered, and ye gave me meat;" (2). "I was thirsty, and ye gave me drink;" (3). "I was a stranger, and ye took me;" (4). "Naked, and ye clothed me;" (5). "I was sick, and ye visited me." The fidelity to detail is marked, and indicates close study on the part of Mr. Frederick Wilson, the designer. There is a delicacy of execution and a strength of expression rarely to be found in works of this character.

This group is under the south gallery and is considered by many to be the finest in the church. In the first is a figure THE representing St. Matthew, and SOUTH ARCADE WINDOWS is a memorial to Benjamin John Cooke (1820-1873); the second is St. Mark, and is in memory of Mary Langley Cooke (1825-1882). Mr. and Mrs. Cooke were the parents of Mr. William L. Cooke, our church treasurer. The third represents St. John, the design being taken from Thorvaldsen's famous statue. It is a memorial to Mary Burnside Morris (1813-1891), the mother of Mr. Charles E. Morris. The fourth contains the figure of St. Luke, and the fifth, that of St. Paul. These last two are memorials to Mr. and Mrs. Jonathan Ogden, the parents of Mr. Robert C. Ogden.

After examining these windows carefully, a gentleman visiting the church said: "I have seen the leading cathedrals of Europe and have closely observed many of the windows, but I have nowhere found finer work in glass than is represented in these five figures of the apostles." All, with the exception of the St. John window, are from originals by Frederick Wilson, and the entire five were executed by the Tiffany Decorative Company.

This fine window is in the north vestibule and represents John the Baptist, with the inscription, '' Prepare ye the way of the Lord.'' The figure of the Baptist has remarkable force and power, and the accessories are in entire accord with the historic surroundings of the subject. It was presented by the Ministering Circle of King's Daughters. A tablet to the memory of Miss Marie Meares, who died January 4, 1897, and who was one of the most faithful and devoted members of this active Circle, is placed on the window.

JOHN THE BAPTIST WINDOW

The windows under the east end of the south gallery were erected by Mr. and Mrs. James C. Taylor to the memory of their four children—Lizzie V., John C., Annie Morris, and Harriet Hollond. These windows were the work of Alfred Godwin, and have for their design lilies and passion flowers, surrounded by beautiful ornamental work.

OTHER WINDOWS

In the lobby leading to the north gallery is an interesting group of four windows, representing St. Michael, St. Raphael, St. Uriel and St. Gabriel. Mr. Wilson, who designed them, and Mr. Godwin, who made them, have reason to be proud of their work. The St. Michael window perpetuates the memory of Mary Elizabeth Blodget (1830-1888); the St. Raphael

JOHN THE BAPTIST WINDOW

window is a memorial to Emma M. Smith,
who died October 3, 1883; the St. Uriel window is in memory of dead members of the
Armstrong Class; and the St. Gabriel window
keeps alive the memory of Samuel B. Stewart,
who was born May 9, 1865, and died September 29, 1885. Young Stewart was a beloved
and faithful worker in the church and school,
and was preparing himself for the work of the
gospel ministry, when the Father called him
to a higher life and a nobler service.

Our church becomes nearer and dearer to us
all as we see on every side these beautiful memorials of a deathless love, through which the
light of heaven falls as a benediction, and by
which we catch faint suggestions of the bright-
ness surrounding those who now walk in " the
city that hath no need of the sun, neither of
the moon, to shine in it, for the glory of God
doth lighten it."

The organ is one of the finest in the city and
was made by Haskell, the famous builder, at a
cost of $8,500. "It is divided
and stands on either side of the
chancel, with the key-box and
choir-seats arranged between.
The separate parts are connected by tubular
pneumatic action. Particular attention has
been paid to the acoustics of the building, and
the position the organ occupies—the strength

THE
ORGAN

of the various qualities of tone being most admirably balanced. The instrument, as a whole, is a representative one of the perfection to which the art of organ-building has been advanced. It is in every way worthy of the edifice in which it stands.

"One of the important features of the instrument is the Haskell patent register keys. This device does away with all draw stop knobs, and, in connection with the Haskell patent combination and crescendo attachment, effects an entirely new and distinct method of registration. The register keys consist of a row of alternate sharps and naturals, of the same scale as the manual key-board; they are situated just above the swell keys. The natural keys bring the stops on and the sharps take them off. By pushing down a natural the stop is drawn and remains down until released by the depression of its corresponding sharp. In this way the player can readily see what stops are on and what are not. The register keys are grouped together to avoid confusion, and each is engraved on the front with the name of the stop which it controls. They can be operated either singly or in combination as desired, as by a single motion of the hand one can be drawn and another pushed off, or a group of stops can be drawn by a single stroke.

NORTH GALLERY LOBBY

" By the application of the patent combination and crescendo attachment, the player obtains a control of the instrument which heretofore has not been attainable, being enabled thereby to bring on or take off any number of stops desired. It also acts as a crescendo, drawing one stop after another until all stops are drawn, and pushing them off in the same manner, without the lifting of a finger from the key-board to effect this orchestral crescendo and diminuendo ; thus effects in registration, which have heretofore been sacrificed for the sake of preserving the harmony of the composition, can be produced without loss of time and wholly without the aid of the hand. Although the resources of this pedal are almost unlimited, its operation is extremely simple.

" On each side of the pedal is a flange, situated in a convenient place to be operated by the toe of the shoe. These flanges bring the crescendo into action—by pressing the one to the left to bring the stops on, and the other to the right to take them off. Any number of stops can be brought on or taken off at once by placing the pedal in position before pressing the flange to the right or left.

" On the main board, over the keys, is an expression indicator which shows the exact position of the pedal, so that the player can tell at a glance how much of the organ would be brought on or taken off by the motion of the foot to the right or left.

"The bellows is fitted with large horizontal acting feeders, which are operated by an eight-inch Ross hydraulic motor, situated in the cellar, thus furnishing a full supply of wind at all times. In this organ each chest is provided with its reservoir, or regulator, giving to each part of the organ the proper pressure, and insuring absolute steadiness in the wind. The scales and voicing of the pipes, on which mainly depend the success of the instrument, are of the highest order of excellence."

The organ has three manuals, thirty-eight speaking stops, with six couplers ; seven combination pedals, a complete pedal scale of thirty notes, and 2314 pipes, ranging in length from two inches to sixteen feet.

Mr. Russell King Miller, son of the Rev. Dr. J. R. Miller, was the organist from the dedication of the building to 1898, when he resigned to accept a similar position in the First Church, Germantown. His successor was Mr. D. E. Crozier, who was the organist of Princeton Chapel during the two years preceding his graduation from the college in 1886. He studied in Chicago under W. S. B. Mathews, and in Paris under Guilmant. From 1886 to his coming to us in 1898, he was the organist of the Market Square Presbyterian Church,

D. E. CROZIER

Harrisburg, Pa. He has exceptional taste and ability, and easily ranks among the foremost performers of the city.

The land (100 feet on Broad street and 200 feet on Federal street, including the entire distance from Broad to Juniper streets), which was secured at different times, cost $21,833.33 ; the building, including complete furnishings, approximates $120,000.00—making a total expenditure, in round numbers, of about $142,000.00. Property has greatly appreciated in value since the land was purchased. It is estimated that the entire plant, including the chapel property, is now worth nearly a quarter of a million of dollars. It is hoped at no distant day to erect a commodious building on the lot back of the church, which shall furnish ample accommodations for the manifold organizations now helping in carrying forward the work.

TOTAL COST OF BUILDING

The following resolution was adopted at a congregational meeting of the Tenth Presbyterian Church, held May 24th, 1893 :

TENTH CHURCH LEGACY

"*Resolved*, That when the property at Twelfth and Walnut streets be sold, $75,000 of the money be appropriated to the Hollond Presbyterian Church—$35,000 of the same to be applied to the payment of the church indebtedness, and $40,000 to be held as an endowment fund, protected by the language of the deed of the Tenth Presbyterian Church, which is as follows : ' Provided . always that they shall adhere to and maintain the mode of faith and church discipline as set forth in the Confession of Faith of the Presbyterian Church in the United States of America.' "

At a congregational meeting of the Hollond Memorial Church, held on the 5th of June, the following action was taken on the resolution adopted by the Tenth Church :

"*Resolved*, That the Harriet Hollond Memorial Presbyterian Church accept the proposal of the Tenth Presbyterian Church to transfer to the use of the Harriet Hollond Memorial Church, from the proceeds of the sale of the property at the north-east corner of Twelfth and Walnut streets, the sum of $75,000, upon the conditions named in the communication containing the proposal, and subject to the language of the deed of the Tenth Presbyterian Church, as follows : ' Provided always that they shall adhere to and maintain the mode of faith and church discipline as set forth in the Confession of Faith of the Presbyterian Church in the United States of America.' " It was further

" *Resolved*, That the thanks of the Hollond Church are due and are hereby tendered to the Tenth Church for the generous Christian spirit displayed in the liberal assistance in the work of the Hollond Church proposed by the Tenth Church in its recent action."

The following extract, relative to the bequest of the Tenth Church, is from the annual report (January, 1896) of Mr. William L. Cooke, our treasurer :

"On April 8th, 1895, the board of trustees of the Hollond Memorial Church received through its treasurer, from the trustees of the Tenth Presbyterian Church, deeds for the chapel property at the corner of Federal and Clarion streets, free of all encumbrance ; a check for $35,000 ; mortgages to the value of $5,500, being the Boardman Trust—also check for $279.40, being the accrued interest on the same to date ; deed for ten burial lots in Woodland Cemetery, and certificate of two shares of stock in the ' Woodland Cemetery Company.' At the same time, the Philadelphia Trust, Safe Deposit and Insurance Company, as trustees, received $40,000 as an endowment fund for the Hollond Church."

In his fourteenth anniversary sermon, delivered on Sunday morning, October 3rd, 1897, Dr. Paden said :

"God has brought our church into a large place. Situated as we are in one of the world's great cities, and at one of the great life-centres of that city, we have a field which is exceeding broad. There are more immortal souls within a half hour's walk of this church than there are scattered over the whole area of a half dozen of our newer western states. Moreover, our force is phenomenally large ; there are as many members in Hollond as there are in the whole twenty-three Presbyterian churches of Utah. As for our church property, it is worth almost as much as all their church property combined. Few congregations in this great and wealthy city have finer accommodations for 'whosoever will,' and none have freer.

"Much of this enlargement has come to us during the last fourteen years. Fourteen years ago, this church did not own an inch of property ; it did not own the building in which it worshiped. The school was still almost entirely supported by the mother church ; some

$1,300 had been raised toward a building fund; this was every dollar of assets the church had in hand ; but she had faith and hope, and the favor of God. This favor was manifested in innumerable ways, most notably in the end by his stirring the workers and the members of the church with the spirit of liberality and by his guidance of the mother church in the making of her last will and testament. Now, our church property and endowment represent capital to the amount of a quarter of a million dollars. We have enough members to fill the church and to carry on its work with notable efficiency, if our people will only rise to their privileges and their possible spiritual power.''

The following figures, taken from the minutes of the General Assembly, show the membership of the church on the first of April of each year since its organization :

1882	259	1891	754
1883	310	1892	775
1884	341	1893	825
1885	360	1894	1,005
1886	460	1895	1,090
1887	502	1896	1,105
1888	562	1897	1,164
1889	660	1898	1,170
1890	697	1899	1,170

Although there has been a net gain of only 6 since the report of 1897, yet 125 persons—71 on profession of faith and 54 by letter—have united with the church since that time. The losses by deaths and removals have almost equalled the gain.

Our growth, when compared with that of other churches, has been gratifying. In 1882, when we had 259 members, there were 41 larger congregations of our Presbytery; in 1883, 36; in 1884, 26; in 1885, 27; in 1886, 20; in 1887, 15; in 1888, 13; in 1889, 9; in 1890, 10; in 1891, 8; in 1892, 7; in 1893, 5; in 1894, 2; in 1895, 2; in 1896, 2; in 1897, 2; in 1898, 1; in 1899, 1.

The following table gives the number of persons received to the church each year :

	On Profession.	By Letter.	Total.
1882	79	19	98
1883	55	21	76
1884	45	18	63
1885	44	21	65
1886	81	42	123
1887	59	31	90
1888	99	33	132
1889	88	43	131
1890	52	26	78
1891	47	36	83
1892	56	35	91
1893	60	15	75
1894	83	92	175
1895	75	49	124
1896	36	29	65
1897	76	43	119
1898	52	20	72
1899	19	34	53
Totals	1,106	607	1,713

It will thus be seen that 1,106 persons have united with the church on profession of faith and 607 by letter, making a total of 1,713. If we add the original membership—229—we have a grand total of 1,942 persons whose names have appeared on our church rolls between March, 1882, and April, 1899. The difference between 1,942, the total membership, and 1,170, the present membership, is 772— the number of names which for various causes has been removed from the roll. In a floating congregation, such as ours, this number is not unduly large. It is pleasant to know that many of those who have removed from us are now giving helpful service to other churches.

203 adults and 571 children have been baptized. The Sunday-school reports this year (1899) a membership of 1,176, making it, with one exception, the largest school of the Presbytery. The total congregational collections aggregate $215,coo.oo.

These figures represent only the *numerical* growth, which, let it never be forgotten, should mean but little in any church when compared with the *spiritual*. The religious organizations, however small in numbers, which laid the foundation of the world-wide usefulness of such men as Moffat and Livingstone, Duff and Brainerd, have been instrumental in rendering an infinitely nobler service to God and to humanity than have those with hundreds of members whose only evidence of Christianity is that their names appear on the church registers. For, after all, it is the upbuilding of Christ-like manhood and womanhood that counts. It is in this direction that Hollond has rendered a far-reaching service. It has never failed in its insistence that for a life to ring true, creed and conduct must go hand in hand. Through its influence, character has been developed, homes have been refined, and social life has grown purer and more wholesome. Eternity alone will reveal the results of the quiet and beautiful ministry of those who have here been taught to stand bravely in life's hard places for " whatsoever things are true."

That the church is dear to many may be inferred from the following portion of a letter recently written by one of its workers :

" What a powerful centre of usefulness our dear Hollond is ! How helpful is the influence of the truly consecrated lives we have in our church family ! The services are reverent and uplifting, and the entire atmosphere a joy and a benediction. It is a holy place—a place for the truly penitent soul to get into close and helpful touch with its Saviour. I am always spiritually stronger after a Sunday of sweet content passed within the walls of our beloved Zion. I am thankful that there are so many good and true friends of Jesus among our members, for I know that he is always present for their sakes, and maybe for the sake also of what I long to be, and because he knows that I have so much need of his presence. My daily prayer is that all of us may so labor that our work may be as lasting as eternity ; that when we shall pass into the great hereafter we may see from the heavenly heights many precious sheaves gathered from our sowing.''

Nor is this feeling confined alone to those who now labor with us; a young lady in a distant city writes :

'' I do not know what the influence was, or wherein lay the charm, but I do know that I always loved and revered my associations with Hollond far above those of any other church. Although I have now been away from it ten years, yet even to this day a great longing possesses me every Sabbath to be there whenever I hear the church bells here ringing. Dear old Hollond ! I wonder if you know just how much your children—whether they be near or far—love you !''

Several of our young men, who received their inspiration and training here and who gave in return much helpful service while they were with us, are now in the gospel ministry, and all have charges. Their names and addresses follow : Rev. Charles A. Oliver, York, Pa.;

Rev. Robert H. Kirk, Coleraine, Pa.; Rev. Peter Rioseco (who is doing an important work as a Sabbath-school missionary of the Presbyterian Board of Publication and Sabbath-school Work) Havana, Cuba; Rev. Samuel Semple, Titusville, Pa.; Rev. W. F. S. Nelson, Ambler, Pa.; Rev. Cleveland Frame, South Hermitage, Pa.; Rev. Charles G. Hopper, Georgetown, Delaware; Rev. Ray H. Carter, assistant pastor of the Walnut Street Church, Philadelphia; Rev. Harry W. Bloch, assistant to Dr. W. M. Paden in the First Presbyterian Church, Salt Lake City, Utah; and Rev. W. H. Dyer, Audenreid, Pa. Although Messrs. Kirk and Rioseco were not members of our church, yet they were so intimately associated with us as to be always included among " our boys."

THEODORE H. LODER

Under God, much of our spiritual and numerical growth was due to the faithful pulpit and pastoral ministrations of Drs. Paden and Miller. With a fidelity seldom excelled, they devoted themselves, to the extent of their ability, to the work, and it is not surprising that they won the love and confidence of all their people.

During the latter part of 1891, Dr. Paden's health became impaired, and early in January, 1892, he was granted by the session a leave of absence of three months, which was afterwards extended to nine, in order that he might recuperate. He spent much of the time in the mountains of North and South Carolina and was greatly benefited. His first sermon, after his return, was delivered in the chapel on the 2d of October. He said in part:

DR. PADEN IN THE SOUTH

"If there was one desire uppermost in my heart as I entered the new year, it was to make it the most active and effective year of my ministry. As a pastor, a preacher, an apostle of good courage, an organizer for the day of church-occupation, and as a useful assistant in the thousand little things which some one must know about in an era of church building, I desired to shoulder and carry my share of the burden. Instead, at the beginning of the year I was laid aside with grippe-pneumonia, and have spent the months for which I had devised unusual industry, in inactivity, while nature made her kindly, but tedious repairs.

"Just now, I would talk about things just ahead, rather than of things just past—with this one exception: I am eager to say that one of the divinest touches which has ever come into my life, has come through your affectionate and prayerful interest in me during these months of absence. None of you will be jealous when I give Dr. Miller the place of honor in this ministry of love. He has served you for me, and me for you; and all of us for Christ in a very Christ-like way. Other loving-kindnesses have come into my life through the wise and prompt provisions made for me by the session; the words of love and good cheer from one and another of the people; and through the Spirit of Love which brought me boundless comfort through my confidence in the unspoken affections of the many whose love has been none the less real because silent."

GEORGE D. MCILVAINE

Dr. Miller was away from the city from March 27, 1893, to the middle of the following May, during which time he enjoyed an extended trip along the Pacific coast.

In the fall of 1895, Dr. Paden received an invitation to spend the winter in Paris for the purpose of taking charge of the DR. PADEN GOES TO PARIS evangelistic movement which had for its main object the reaching of the English and American art students in the Latin Quarter of that city. At first, he virtually refused to consider the proposition, deeming it inexpedient to leave the work of Hollond even for a season; but after much conference, he finally determined to accept. The session took the following action:

WHEREAS, Rev. Wm. M. Paden, D.D., has been invited to take charge of highly important evangelical work among the American and English students in Paris for six months from the 1st of December prox.; and

WHEREAS, A careful examination by the pastors and session of the opportunities thus afforded indicates hopeful promise of large influence for good; and

WHEREAS, Dr. Paden is inclined to enter upon the work if it appears possible to do so without impairing the efficiency and usefulness of the Hollond Memorial Church. Therefore it is

Resolved, That in the opinion of this session it is possible to carry out the plan suggested in

the foregoing preamble, and therefore that Rev.
Dr. Paden is granted a six months' leave of
absence from the pastorate of the Hollond
Memorial Church, the dates of such absence
to be determined by his own convenience; and
it is further

Resolved, That Mr. W. H. Dyer be employed to assist Rev. Dr. Miller in the additional pastoral work during and caused by the
absence of Dr. Paden, and that Dr. Paden's
place in the pulpit be filled by the engagement
of other clergymen as supplies.

Dr. Paden sailed for Paris on the 21st of
November, 1895, and returned on the 5th of
June, 1896. Dr. Miller, who spent July and
August, 1896, in Europe, thus wrote: '' It was
very pleasant in Paris to hear good reports of
Dr. Paden's work among the students. Most
of those who attended his services are now
away from their artist haunts, but I had the
pleasure of meeting with two or three of them,
and was delighted to hear them speak so gratefully of Dr. Paden and so confidently of the
value of his work and influence. Dr. Thurber,
pastor of the American Chapel, spoke without
stint of the value of Dr. Paden's services.'' ·

During Dr. Paden's absence, Dr. Miller received invaluable assistance in the pastoral
work from Mr. W. H. Dyer, a member of
Hollond, and at that time a student in Princeton Theological Seminary. He greatly endeared himself to the people by his faithful

CHARLES HUNTER

H. P. FORD

and sympathetic devotion to the work. During Dr. Miller's absence in Europe, he continued to assist Dr. Paden.

Among the prominent clergymen who appeared in our pulpit while Dr. Paden was away, were Dr. Theodore L. Cuyler, Brooklyn, New York; Dr. L. Y. Graham, Philadelphia; Dr. J. R. Danforth, Philadelphia; Dr. Charles A. Dickey, Philadelphia; Dr. James O. Murray, dean of Princeton University; Mr. Robert E. Speer, secretary of the Board of Foreign Missions; Dr. Charles Wood, Philadelphia; Rev. Charles A. Oliver, York, Pa.; Dr. J. F. Dripps, Germantown, Pa.; Dr. Arthur J. Brown, secretary of the Board of Foreign Missions; Dr. William R. Taylor, of the Brick Church, Rochester, New York; Dr. S. W. Dana, Philadelphia; Dr. Maltbie D. Babcock, of the Brown Memorial Church, Baltimore, Md.; Dr. Alexander McKenzie, Cambridge, Mass.; Rev. Stephen B. Penrose, president of Whitman College, Washington; Dr. J. D. Moffatt, president of Washington and Jefferson College, Washington, Pa.; Rev. Henry E. Cobb, of the Collegiate Reformed Church, New York, and Dr. William Brenton Greene, Jr., of Princeton Theological Seminary.

It is but just to state that it was expressly stipulated by Dr. Paden that the expenses incurred for pastoral assistance and for pulpit supplies during his absence in Paris should be paid out of his salary account, which was done.

The year 1897 brought to the work its most serious losses.   In April, Mr. Robert C. Ogden, whose business required him to

THE LOSSES be permanently in New York, re-
OF 1897   signed the superintendency of the school.   He had given to it eighteen years of the most faithful and helpful service.   Other losses were to follow—the resignations of Drs. Paden and Miller.

Dr. Paden spent his summer vacation of that year in Utah, and during his visit preached in the First Presbyterian Church of Salt Lake City.   Soon after his return he received a call from that church to come to it as its pastor. After careful consideration of all the interests involved, he determined to accept the call. This decision he announced from the pulpit on Sunday morning, October 3d—his fourteenth anniversary as the pastor of Hollond.

The next day Presbytery took the following action:

"At a meeting of the Presbytery of Philadelphia, held October 4, 1897, the Rev. William M. Paden, D.D., presented a request for the dissolution of his pastoral relations to the Hollond Memorial Church.   Whereupon it was

"*Resolved*, That the congregation of the Hollond Memorial Church be, and the same

CHARLES A. CHEW

are hereby cited to appear by commissioners duly appointed, at a meeting of the Presbytery to be held in the Assembly Room, 1334 Chestnut street, on Monday, October 18, 1897, at 2 o'clock, to show cause, if any there be, why Dr. Paden's request be not granted.''

On the 14th of October Dr. Miller sent to the session the following letter:

'' My relation as a worker in the Hollond Memorial Presbyterian Church had its origin in an invitation from the boards of the church. It has reference only to the pastorate of Dr. Paden. If therefore Dr. Paden's resignation be accepted, my relation to the church is at the same time ended without any motion of mine.

'' But to remove all uncertainty in the matter, I hereby tender to the session my resignation, to take effect on and after next Sabbath, October 17th.

''I would have it understood also that this severance of relations on my part is final; that I could not consent to return to any pastoral relation in the church. The nature of my other duties to the Church at large, in my editorial position in the Board of Publication, devolves upon me ever-increasing burden and responsibility, making it impossible for me to assume again the additional labors of a pastorate or co-pastorate.

'' Any assistance, however, which I can

render the Hollond Church in securing another pastor, I will cheerfully give. Any visiting of the sick, burying of the dead, or other such ministries as I can perform, until a new pastor is installed, I shall gladly render.

"I must thank the session, the other church boards, and the people of Hollond, for the courtesy and affection which I have received during all these years of my connection with the work. I have tried to do my duty, but no one can be so conscious of the inadequacy of my service as I am myself.

"While I shall no longer have any official connection with the church, I shall never cease to have the warmest affection for it and the deepest interest in its growth and prosperity. I have put too much love and toil and prayer into my nearly seventeen years in Hollond, ever to forget the church.

"I shall cherish the memory of these years of close fellowship with Dr. Paden. For ten years he was a member of my own family and we shall always hold him in most kindly regard. My prayers will rise to God for him in his new home and work, and I shall be affectionately interested in his personal happiness and in the prosperity of the important work to which he believes he has been so clearly called of God."

A congregational meeting, to take action on

CHARLES A. HOEHLING

Dr. Paden's request, was held in the chapel on Friday evening, October 15th.

CONGREGA-TIONAL MEETING Dr. William H. Gill, at the request of the session, acted as moderator. Dr. Paden spoke briefly as follows:

"On Sunday week I tried to make it clear that my request to be released was not due to any lack of confidence in this field; it is one of the very best in the city, a church set on a fruitful hill. It is in good financial condition, and is in every way a desirable charge. I want you to understand that I do not resign in a fit of discouragement; that I am not trying to get away from a church that I feel has reached its best. I want to leave you full of courage as to the undeveloped capacity of this field.

"I tried, in the second place, to have you understand clearly that I do not go, or ask you to release me, because I distrust you, or the loyalty or love of the members, or any of the members, of this congregation; and I want to emphasize, *that least of all do I distrust the loyalty and love of the session of this congregation, for our records will show that for fourteen years there has not been a divided vote.*

"The next Sabbath I tried to show to you the other side—the overmastering reason I had for going. I tried to give you a glimpse of what I considered to be providential indica-

tions that my going west is a part of God's
plan for my life.

"My conscience is perfectly clear on this
subject. I cannot be true to my conscience
without hearing the 'Woe be unto me' if I
obey not this call, which I have every reason
to believe to be the voice of God.

"I simply ask that you join with me in requesting my release of Presbytery, in order
that I may obey these beckonings of providence. Only a glimpse of these beckonings
have been given to you, because God's dealings are very personal with man. I simply
ask that you will trust me, and trust God's
providence. Never once in these fourteen
years has this congregation said 'no' to anything for which I asked. And you will understand, I think, that this is a matter which is
more personal to me than anything I have ever
asked of you before; and I say that the way
in which you can best show your confidence in
the saneness of my judgment, in the sincerity
of my desires to follow conscience, and what I
believe to be the voice of God—the best way
in which you can show your affection for me,
the best way and clearest way, is by joining
with me in asking for my release.

"Yes, there is one way that is better; there
is one way that you can show your loyalty and
love to me better, and that is *by standing by*

GEORGE H. KELLY

*this work after you have released me, and I am
gone.*

"God grant that the future of Hollond may
be the best testimony that could possibly be
made to the fact that good work has been done
here during the past!"

Mr. W. L. Cooke read the following resolutions, addressed to the Presbytery of Philadelphia, which were adopted by a standing vote
—no one speaking or voting against them:

1.   That we hereby acquiesce with Dr. Paden in his
request that the pastoral relations between himself
and this congregation be dissolved.

2.   That we take this action with unfeigned reluc-
tance and deepest regret, not of any voluntary motion
or desire on our part, but because of Dr. Paden's
insistence that it should be done, he having both pri-
vately and from the pulpit declared it to be his solemn conviction that it is his duty to accept the call
recently tendered him by the First Presbyterian
Church in Salt Lake City, Utah.

3.   That in taking this action, the Hollond Memorial Presbyterian Church and congregation hereby desire to express their very high appreciation of Dr.
Paden as a man, a Christian, a preacher and pastor,
and as a man of high literary culture and attainments,
and to bear testimony to the sincere affection and
respect with which he is universally regarded, not
only by the people of his immediate flock, but by the
community at large.

4.   That we take pleasure in bearing testimony to
the success of his ministry amongst us both from a
material and spiritual point of view.   When Dr. Paden

was settled over us as pastor fourteen years ago, the membership of our church was hardly more than three hundred, while at the present time it numbers nearly twelve hundred ; and it has been during his administration also, and owing in a goodly measure to his persevering efforts, that our house of worship on Broad street has been erected.   No one has recognized more generously than Dr. Paden that, in carrying forward all this great work to its present prosperous condition, he has been ably seconded by the Rev. J. R. Miller, D.D., who, at the request of the session, has been associated with him during nearly the whole of his pastorate, and whose services on behalf of the church have been as unremitting as they have been invaluable, the two striving together for the glory of God in the upbuilding of Hollond.

5.   That in parting with Dr. Paden, whom we love, our sorrow and perplexity are rendered all the greater because the nature of the relation existing between him and Dr. Miller, whom we also love, is such that the severance of the one tie carries with it and involves the severance of the other, so that we are, as it were, bereft of two pastors at one stroke, leaving us a pastorless flock, as sheep without a shepherd.   Nevertheless, we face the future hopefully, confident that He, whose work it is, will constantly watch over us, and in his own good time send us another or others of his servants, who will take the oversight of the flock and give to the work a still greater enlargement than it has even now attained.

6.   That we will ever cherish the most grateful recollections of these years of unwearied and self-denying labors for Hollond on the part of both these beloved brethren; that we will enshrine them both in our hearts and remember them in our prayers, praying that they may long be spared, each in his own

AMOS DOTTERER

sphere, to aid in the upbuilding and extension of the Redeemer's kingdom; and for Dr. Paden, whose call removes him not only from our church but from our city, that a success even greater than that he has achieved here in Philadelphia may crown his labors in Utah, or wherever God in his providence may order his lot.

7. That Messrs. John Russell, H. P. Ford, W. J. Barr, T. H. Lodor, and W. L. Cooke be, and hereby are appointed commissioners to represent this church and congregation, and to present this action to the Presbytery.

In closing the meeting Dr. Gill said :

" It has been my pleasure on more than one occasion to speak of Hollond as a united congregation. I have not heard a single word of dissension against this people by anyone. It is a very great record for any congregation that is so large, with two pastors associated together for fourteen years, to be at peace among themselves, to be in harmony and accord as brethren in the Lord. As you love your Saviour, as you serve your God, stand by each other, stand by your Master, stand by the church, and God will take care of you. It is God's church, and his work. He sympathizes with you, and he will see that the work goes on. Workmen may die, men may come and go, but the work goes on forever—at least until the purposes for which the Church has been constituted in the world, have been accomplished.''

On Monday afternoon, October 18th, Presbytery reluctantly acquiesced in the request for a dissolution of the pastoral relationship existing between Dr. Paden and the church.   Mr. W. L. Cooke, presented the resolutions adopted at the congregational meeting, and made a short address, expressive of the devotion of the people to Dr. Paden, and of their sorrow and deep sense of loss at his going from them.   Brief remarks along the same line were also made by the other three commissioners present—Messrs. Theodore H. Loder, H. P. Ford, and John Russell.   Addresses full of regret, commendation, and high personal regard, were made by the Rev. Drs. A. J. Sullivan, W. H. Gill, H. A. Nelson, M. J. Hyndman, J. G. Bolton, J. A. Henry, W. M. Rice, and others.

ACTION OF PRESBYTERY

"There is no man," said Dr. Paden, "to whom I would more willingly commit the work of Hollond at this time than to Dr. Miller.   I most earnestly and heartily unite with the session in asking that he be appointed moderator of the church until a pastor be chosen."

Presbytery granted the request.   The Rev. Dr. Gill was appointed to preach on the following Sabbath, and to declare the pulpit vacant.

By a standing vote, Presbytery adopted the following :

JAMES C. TAYLOR

Resolved, That we place upon record our sincere regret at the departure of the Rev. Dr. Paden from the Presbytery ; that we hereby express our high appreciation of his eminent Christian character ; his ability as a preacher, pastor and presbyter ; that we shall follow him with our prayers and best wishes for his success to his new field of labor.

Dr. Paden preached his last sermon as the pastor of Hollond on Sunday evening, October 17th, his text being "*For I am* DR. PADEN'S *persuaded that neither death, nor* LAST *life * * * shall be able to separate* SERMON *us from the love of God.*" Romans 8 : 38–39. The church was crowded. On the following Wednesday evening, the Ushers' Association tendered him a farewell reception in the chapel. People were in line until nearly eleven o'clock waiting for an opportunity to take him by the hand, to express their sorrow at his going, and to wish him Godspeed in his new field of labor.

Dr. W. H. Gill preached at both services on Sunday, October 24th. Just before he announced his morning text, he THE PULPIT said: "I am here at the request of DECLARED the session and by appointment of VACANT Presbytery, to inform this congregation officially that the request of Dr. Paden— that the pastoral relation existing between him and this church be dissolved—has been granted.

I now officially declare this pulpit to be vacant."

By virtue of his appointment by Presbytery as moderator of the Hollond session, Dr. Miller continued to perform all pastoral duties until the pulpit should be filled. Steps were at once taken to secure a pastor. Several committees, consisting of representative men of the congregation, visited nearby cities to hear able ministers ; a number of clergymen, who were preaching as supplies in other pulpits in this city, were also heard. No recommendations, however, were made.

SEEKING A PASTOR

Dr. George Edward Martin preached twice in our pulpit on Sunday, April 24, 1898. He also conducted both services on Sunday, May 1st. At a congregational meeting held in the chapel on the 10th of May, he received a unanimous call to the pastorate. Messrs. William L. Cooke, William J. Barr, Charles A. Hoehling, John Russell and Daniel J. Weaver, were appointed commissioners to present the call to Presbytery.

DR. MARTIN CALLED

Dr. Miller preached his last sermon on Sunday evening, June 5th, his subject being, " Into Thine Hands." Psalm 31 : 5. The church was filled with a deeply interested and attentive congregation. This serv-

DR. MILLER'S LAST SERMON

WILLIAM J. BARR

ice witnessed the close of a long and faithful ministry.

On Sunday morning, June 12th, Dr. Martin again preached, and at this service announced his acceptance of the DR. MARTIN'S call which had been extended to ACCEPTANCE him by the congregation ; it being understood that he would not enter upon his pastoral work until September.

Dr. J. B. Brandt, pastor of the Tyler Place Presbyterian Church, St. Louis, Mo., had charge of the work during the month of July, and by his genial, kindly nature made many friends among the people. He received valuable assistance from the Rev. Harry W. Bloch, who was very helpful both in the church and school work during the summer. After Dr. Brandt's departure, the pulpit was supplied by the Rev. Harry Bloch, Dr. Frederick J. Stanley, of Atlantic City, N. J., Dr. C. S. Sargent, of St. Louis, Mo., Rev. A. B. Robinson, editor of the Church at Home and Abroad, and Dr. George S. Chambers, of Harrisburg, Pa.

Dr. Martin was installed pastor of Hollond on the 17th of October, 1898. Dr. S. W. Dana, pastor of the Walnut Street DR. MARTIN'S Church, presided and proposed INSTALLATION the constitutional questions; Rev. E. P. Terhune, D. D., preached

the sermon ; Dr. Samuel A. Mutchmore, *
editor of *The Presbyterian*, delivered the charge
to the people; Dr. Charles A. Dickey gave the
charge to the pastor, and Dr. J. R. Miller
made the installation prayer.

On the Wednesday evening following the
installation the Ushers' Association gave Dr.
and Mrs. Martin a reception in the chapel.

The Rev. L. L. Overman accepted an invitation to become Dr. Martin's assistant. He
was in the pulpit for the first
REV. LESLIE L. time on December 5, 1898, and
OVERMAN assisted in the service. His first
sermon was preached January 8,
1899, his text being '' And he spake this par-
able unto certain which trusted in themselves
that they were righteous, and despised others.''
Luke 18 : 9.

It is earnestly hoped that under these our
new leaders, our beloved church will go forward to greater spiritual power and ever-increasing usefulness.

---

* Dr. Mutchmore came from a sick bed to take part in the installation service. He had been in poor health for some time.
His death took place thirteen days later—October 30th. On
Sunday evening, May 26, 1861, on the invitation of the Rev.
Dr. W. M. Rice, he preached his first sermon in Philadelphia in
the old Moyamensing chapel in Carpenter street. Thus by a
singular providence, his first and last sermons in Philadelphia,
although delivered more than a generation apart, were preached
in the Hollond field.

ANDREW R. POULSON

The officials of the church at the present time are :

Pastor

Rev. George Edward Martin, D. D.

Assistant

Rev. Leslie L. Overman

Elders

Robert C. Ogden	William L. Cooke
Theodore H. Loder	George D. McIlvaine
Henry A. Walker	

Deacons

Charles Hunter	George H. Kelly
Charles A. Chew	Charles A. Hoehling
H. P. Ford	

Trustees

Robert C. Ogden	Theodore H. Loder
William L. Cooke	William J. Barr
Amos Dotterer	Henry A. Walker
James C. Taylor	Andrew R. Poulson
H. P. Ford	

Treasurer

William L. Cooke

Janitor

George W. Taylor

Hollond owes much to its Sunday-school, from which it had its origin. But for the devotion of Miss Estabrook, Miss Penrose and Mr. Beadle, and the faithfulness of a number of little children away back in October, 1865 (see chapter entitled " The New Life "), it is doubtful whether our church would be in existence to-day.

To the school belongs the honor also of making the first attempt to raise money for the new church building. Through " brickbooks," and other means, $898.76 had been collected as early as November, 1882.

The additions to the church membership come largely from the school, and from those who are influenced by the teachers and scholars, supplemented by the earnest efforts of the pastors.

Then, too, through the generosity of the school, the church is represented in a number of benevolent enterprises, thus bringing it into prominence as a liberal supporter of worthy charity. Among the objects to which it has

WILLIAM L. COOKE

contributed comparatively recently may be mentioned the Young Men's Christian Association (South Branch), the Boards of Church Erection, Home Missions, Education, Ministerial Relief, and Publication and Sabbath-school Work ; Presbyterian Hospital, Presbyterian Home for Aged Couples and Old Men, Seaside Home, Visiting Nurses' Society, State Sunday-school Association, Midnight Mission, Hampton Institute, French and Waldensian Missions, Consumptives' Home, Presbyterian Orphanage, Mariners' Church, Armenian Relief, Whitman College, Children's Aid Society, Magdalen Society, Albert Barnes Memorial, Seamen's Mission, and Lincoln University.

It would be pleasant, if it were possible, to record the names of all those who have taught in the school—some for a brief season only, others through many years. The sand-dunes on the New Jersey seaboard, although nameless and constantly changing, are quite as effective in keeping back the destroying waves of the ocean as are, on other sea-coasts, the giant rocks whose names are world-wide ; and so the transient and forgotten teachers who have labored with us have, in their way and for the time being, doubtless been as forceful in helping to stay the waves of sin as have those who are known to us all through their long and splendid service—" To every man his work."

We are grateful to one and to all who have in
any way contributed to the usefulness of the
school.

A full list of the officers and teachers of 1876
appears on pages 49-50 ; a list of the present
teaching force will close this chapter.   For the
purpose of comparison, the names of the officers and teachers of 1887 (a period about half-
way between 1876 and 1899) are herewith
given : Superintendent, Robert C. Ogden ; associate superintendents, William L. Cooke and
Henry A. Walker ; treasurer, William L. Du-
Bois ; missionary treasurer, Samuel R. Sharp ;
statistical secretaries, Daniel J. Weaver and
William B. Hens ; librarians, James A. Main,
Thomas Harkness, Charles V. Williams, Samuel
Brown.   Teacher of Primary Department, Miss
Minnie Sherwood; teachers of Junior Depart-
ment, Miss Sallie Cooke and Miss Mary J. Col-
well ; teachers of Main School, William L. Du-
Bois, Prof. Edward MacHarg, Miss Elizabeth
Potts, Mrs. Charles E. Morris, Rev. William
M. Paden, D. D., Rev. J. R. Miller, D. D.,
Samuel R. Sharp, Theodore H. Loder, Mrs. R.
D. Clark, Miss Lydia S. Penrose, Miss Mary
E. Hill, Samuel M. Kennedy, Miss Fannie
Fithian, Miss Caroline A. Douglas, Miss Eliz-
abeth L. Pinkerton, Mrs. A. C. Windle, James
Whyte, Wm. J. McLaughlin, Miss Katie B.
Davis, Charles Hamilton, Miss Kate Beard,

Miss Jane MacHarg, David Glandfield, Miss
K. A. Austin, Miss Mamie McCorkell, Henry
A. Walker, T. Miller Plowman, Samuel O.
Walker, Miss Sadie Fleming, Charles A. Chew,
Morris S. Hamilton, Miss M. E. Lennington,
Miss Alice Douglas, Miss Helen Merrick, Miss
Ida Blodget, Miss A. B. Spear, Miss Julia Og-
den, Mrs. Mary V. Mitchell, Gilbert Elliott,
Miss Mary A. Jones, Mrs. Jane Skerritt, Miss
Jennie Crosgrave, H. P. Ford, Mrs. J. R.
Miller, Miss Addie Cooper, Miss Harriet Scott,
Miss S. H. Chew, Miss Emma Bryant, Miss A.
C. Woods, Miss Lizzie Henry, Miss Laura
Penn, Mrs. Mary Furber, Miss Lizzie Holland,
Miss Elizabeth P. Cresswell, Miss Stella White,
Miss Helen Ogden, Mrs. Kate Robinson,
Madame Fillot, Miss S. M. Bloch, and Miss
Elizabeth Rivell. Eighteen of these workers
are still connected with the school.

Mr. Robert C. Ogden, who in 1879 was
elected to the office of superintendent, made
vacant by the death of Mr Charles E. Morris,
was broad-minded, enthusiastic and generous.
Under his wise leadership the school continued
to grow in numbers and efficiency, and its high
standard was maintained.

Many will remember with pleasure the
'' Flower Mission,'' which was introduced into
the school by Mr. Ogden about 1882, ''to encourage the cultivation of flowers as a means of

spiritual growth.'' Flower seeds were given out in the spring and an exhibition held in the fall. Prizes were awarded for the best single plants, the largest collection of plants, and for the best bouquet, basket, or collection of flowers. '' The movement was found to be of value in many ways—in giving pleasure and instruction ; in the refining of taste ; in a beautiful ministry to the sick ; in bringing the scholars together for other than the ordinary Sunday-school purposes ; and in the practical demonstration that Christian work has a right to make use of anything that tends to brighten life's hard places and to broaden humanity.'' For years afterwards flowers found their way weekly to the superintendent's desk (due largely to Mr. Ogden's liberality), and at the close of the session were taken to sick scholars, to whom they were a blessed and beautiful bond of union between themselves and the school.

The '' Boys' Nobility Club '' was instituted by Mr. Ogden in the fall of 1890, '' to cultivate noble ideas of living in the minds of the Hollond boys.'' In order to encourage the boys to familiarize themselves with stories of heroic actions, prizes were awarded to those submitting, at a specified time, the best papers containing ten incidents representing to their minds the noblest deeds of heroism.

HENRY A. WALKER

In February, 1895, an appeal for help was received from the Mizpah Presbyterian Sunday-school, Eighth and Wolf streets. Hollond responded in a very practical way by sending a number of workers to act as teachers. Among these were Miss Bella Chalker, Miss Hattie Ramsay, Miss Marie C. Sutphin, Miss Tillie McKinley, Miss Elizabeth McKinley, Miss Cora S. German, Miss Margaret Burns, Miss Bertha Coward, Mr. and Mrs. Huntley Murdock, Mr. Charles K. Gibson, and Mr. Robert G. Maguire. Of these teachers, Mr. Thomas Gamon, the then superintendent of Mizpah, wrote : '' The homes of many of these devoted workers are quite a distance from the school ; yet, with very few exceptions, not a Sunday has been missed, but, wet or dry, cold or hot, pleasant or otherwise, these friends are always at their post of duty.'' After rendering valuable assistance for a time, these teachers finally returned to Hollond.

For years Mr. Ogden personally gave rewards of books, etc., for faithful attendance on the sessions of the school, and many fine records were made by teachers and scholars. It frequently happened that the number of those who had been absent but two Sundays or less during the year approached one hundred.

The annual excursions to pleasant country places are very popular. They afford an ex-

cellent opportunity for the church and school
to unite with each other for a day of gladness
in "God's first temples"—the woods. Class
picnics and other outings are also frequently
held during the summer months.

Much is made of the Christmas entertainment, at which time the chapel is always pret-
tily festooned with evergreens, and some form
of amusement provided. Giving, not get-
ting, however, is the uppermost thought in the
minds of all. The teachers and children bring
whatever they think will prove useful to the
needy—groceries, vegetables, baskets of provisions, toys, money, subscriptions to magazines, and orders for coal. These are assigned
either by the donors themselves or by a committee specially appointed for that purpose.
Through this generous custom nearly two hundred families, many of them not connected
with our church, annually receive a bit of
Christmas cheer and blessing.

Special attention has always been given to
our Primary and Junior Departments, they
being important factors in replenishing the
class forms of the Main School. Miss Cooke
has been for many years at the head of the
Junior Department, and has given to it faithful and conscientious service. The teachers of
the Primary Department also are devoted to
their important work.

Both Dr. Paden and Dr. Miller taught in the school during their connection with the church. Dr. Paden had charge of the young men's class in the west gallery, now taught by Mr. Overman; and Dr. Miller taught the young ladies' class which occupied the east gallery. This class numbered 275 members. It contributed largely to the building fund of the new church, and in many other ways materially increased the effectiveness of the school. The class is now taught by Mrs. George E. Martin.

The school has quite a large library. A number of the books were presented by Dr. Miller. A large addition was made to it from the Sunday-school library of the old Tenth Church upon the dissolution of that organization.

Our book of worship, for which we are indebted to Mr. Ogden, is, perhaps, one of the best Sunday-school books in existence. It was compiled, under his direct supervision, for our special use, and contains eight "Orders of Service," which may be varied indefinitely by the use of the additional seventeen "Selections from the Psalms." The book also contains 163 hymns, all of which are of exceptional merit.

After each session of the school, some of the teachers linger for a few moments to attend the helpful prayer-meeting, at which earnest peti-

tions are offered to God for his blessings to fall
upon the work of the afternoon, and for the
seed sown in the hearts of the scholars to be
quickened into rich spiritual life. It is a reverent and stimulating service.

A monthly teachers' meeting is held, at
which the affairs of the school are freely discussed, and suggestions, having for their object
the improvement of the school, offered. At
some of these gatherings tea is served, and this
never fails to add a delightful social flavor to
the meetings.

For many years special emphasis has been
placed by our leaders on the necessity of a
careful study of the lesson on the part of the
teachers. In order to encourage such study,
weekly teachers' meetings have long been an
important feature of the work. Until somewhat recently these meetings were held in the
chapel parlor ; they are now held in the hall of
the South Branch Young Men's Christian Association, where not only our own teachers but
those of neighboring churches enjoy the privilege. For many years this class was taught by
Dr. Miller. He relinquished the work only on
severing his connection with the Hollond field.

On the 4th of April, 1879, the school
met with a serious loss in the resignation of
Mr. Robert C. Ogden. On that day he occupied the desk as our leader for the last

WILLIAM L. DuBois

time, and in his accustomed address on the lesson made no allusion whatever to the fact that the close of the session would also witness the close of his official connection with the school. He ended his splendid service of eighteen years with no self-laudation, with no mawkish sentimentality, with no undignified allusions to his noble record. He went from us as quietly as he had done on hundreds of other Sunday afternoons, and in his going only the teachers and a few of the scholars knew of the almost irreparable loss which had come upon us. His letter of resignation, dated April 4th, was received and accepted by the teachers at their meeting on the following evening. It had long been known that his business relations with Wanamaker's New York establishment, of which he was the head, would, sooner or later, compel him to give up the superintendency of the school, and the teachers were in a measure prepared for the letter. It was, however, with unfeigned regret that they acceded to its request. One paragraph of his letter was as follows :

" It is impossible to refer at length to the happy associations in the Hollond school—to its vicissitudes, anxieties, failures, and successes. The officers and teachers do not need any assurance from me of sympathy and regard. An expression of my gratitude would be equally superfluous. The many years of comradeship have made an understanding that is beyond verbal statement.''

The following action was taken by the officers and teachers:

"*Resolved*, That in accepting the resignation of Mr. Robert C. Ogden, superintendent of the school for the past eighteen years, we hereby express our sincere regret that circumstances over which he has no control have compelled him to sever his connection with our school. His loss will be the more felt when we remember his worth as a man, his ability as a teacher, his effectiveness as a speaker, the urbanity of his manner, and his activity and benevolence as a Christian. He carries with him to his new sphere of usefulness the highest regards and best wishes of us all.''

Mr. Ogden's fine personality, uncompromising integrity and masterful strength of character exercised a strong, uplifting influence on the members of the school. He raised the standard of manhood, and gave to the work an added dignity. Life to many means more of earnestness, of self-reliance, and of faithful endeavor because of his kindly presence among us.

Mr. William L. Cooke, who became the associate superintendent under Mr. Charles E. Morris in 1871, had temporary charge of the school after Mr. Ogden's resignation, until

November 1, 1897, when he was elected, against his earnest protest, to the superintendency, a position which he has continued to fill with unwavering fidelity. Mr. Henry A. Walker, his associate in the work since October, 1886, gives invaluable assistance in helping to maintain order, and in seeing that classes are supplied with teachers.

The officers and teachers at the present time are : Superintendent, William L. Cooke ; associate superintendent, Henry A. Walker ; Sabbath-school treasurer, Wm. L. DuBois ; missionary treasurer, John Russell ; recording secretary, Robert G. Maguire ; statistical secretaries, Wm. B. Hens, T. Ellwood Frame, Geo. Rhea Carr, John C. Heil ; distributing secretaries, Wm. H. Fulmer, Wm. E. Thompson, Warren P. Dexter ; librarians, A. W. Martin, J. T. Williams, Wm. Macpherson, R. B. Parsons; leader of singing, Frank S. Holloway ; organist, Miss Tillie Keller ; cornetist, Asher H. Frame ; violinist, Chester Griesemer.

Door-keepers—William McFarland, A. H. Kruse, Wm. Moeller. Teachers of Primary Department—Miss Josephine A. Bloch, Miss Martha J. Crowe, Miss Bessie G. Overbeck, Miss Anne P. Gamon. Teachers of Junior Department—Miss Cooke, Miss Tillie McKinley, Miss Emma P. Blume. Teachers of Main School — John Russell, H. P. Ford, Miss

Elizabeth Potts, Mrs. E. B. Morris, Theodore
H. Loder, Mrs. George Edward Martin, Major
George Gow, Miss Lydia S. Penrose, Mrs.
Mary B. S Fox, Henry A. Walker, Miss
Alice F. Douglas, Thomas Gamon, Miss Leah
Welsh, Miss E. L. Pinkerton, Miss Bertha
Sutphin, Miss Laura Hurgeton, Miss Katie
Davis, Frank L. Hansen, Mrs. Rebecca C.
McVickar, Walter J. Whitaker, Huntley R.
Murdock, Miss Margaret Auld, Miss Mattie
Patton, James F. Wallace, Miss Jane L. Ham-
ilton, George D. McIlvaine, Miss Ida Bloch,
Miss Sara Eddie, Robert G. Maguire, Miss
Mary Niven, Miss Mabel H. Briscoe, William
L. DuBois, Mrs. W. H. Gill, Mrs. M. V.
Mitchell, Miss Anna E. Blume, F. M. Brasel-
mann, Miss Minnie I. Taylor, Miss Sara Barst-
ler, Miss Sara J. Hanna, Miss Harriet Scott,
Miss Annie Kennedy, Miss Mary B. Allen,
Miss Harriet K. Hopkins, Miss Margaretta B.
Morris, Miss M. A. Dickson, Mrs. George D.
McIlvaine, Mrs. Catharine S. Tomlinson,
Mrs. Etta Harpel, Miss Margaret Burns, Miss
Isabella Chalker, Miss Elizabeth Rivell, Miss
Margaret Welsh, Frank R. Buckalew, Rev.
L. L. Overman, Miss Tillie McKinney, Miss
Mary Macpherson, James H. Taitt, and
Samuel H. Barstler. Substitute teachers—
Benjamin F. Lutton, Robert H. Preston, Miss
Margaret M. Smith, Mrs. Mary McAllister,

ROBERT G. MAGUIRE

Miss Mattie McFadden, Miss Mary Murphy, Daniel B. McAllister and Prof. Edward Mac-Harg. As teacher, substitute teacher, and recording secretary, Prof. MacHarg has rendered valuable service to the school for many years.

Of the seventy officers and teachers connected with the school in 1876, six only are now actively engaged in the work—William L. Cooke, Miss Cooke, Miss L. S. Penrose, William L. DuBois, Miss Elizabeth Potts, and Miss Elizabeth Rivell. Miss Rivell was one of the charter members of the Moyamensing Church, and has always been devotedly attached to the work.

Attention has been given at various times to many plans which have had in them promise of usefulness in the development of the church and school; some were temporary expedients, others obtained a permanent place in the work. Among those which have been, or still are, more or less influential for good, may be mentioned the Young Men's Improvement Society, Young People's Pastors' Aid, Pastors' Ladies' Aid Society, Kitchen Garden Class (the first of the kind in Philadelphia), Sewing School, Mothers' Meeting, Parents' and Children's Meeting, Boys' Lyceum, Gospel Links (a temperance organization), Wadsworth Debating and Literary Club, Young Men's Prayer and Conference Meeting, Young Men's Union, Brotherhood of Andrew and Philip, King's Daughters, King's Sons, Woman's Home and Foreign Missionary Society, Boys' and Girls' Mission Band, Young Ladies' Mission Band, Little Light Bearers (a mission band for children under five years), Boys' Brigade, Literary Circle, Fifteen Club (also a literary circle),

Chatauqua Circle, Young People's Association, Christian Endeavor Society, Junior Endeavor Society, University Lectures, Young Men's Christian Association, Athletic Association, Ushers' Association, Choir, Beneficial Society, Building Association, Conference of Workers, Organ Vesper Services, and Normal Class.

It seems well to give a more extended outline of some of the present working forces.

We have always been proud of our volunteer chorus Choir.   It is an organization on which depends much of the effectiveness of the Sunday worship. The members are faithful in the performance of their duties —often at a considerable sacrifice of time and of self.   Mr. Theodore H. Loder was for many years the devoted leader.   On entering the new church in the autumn of 1893, the Choir was re-organized and greatly enlarged under the supervision of Mr. Russell King Miller, who occupied the dual position of organist and musical director until 1895, when Mr. Charles M. Schmitz became musical director, Mr. Miller continuing as organist.   Mr. Schmitz served with entire acceptance until June, 1897, when, to the regret of all, he relinquished his position.   The members of the Choir presented him with a complimentary letter setting forth their appreciation of his services.

THE CHURCH CHOIR

Mr. Miller again resumed the duties of musical director in addition to his work as organist —a position he continued to hold until the 7th of August, 1898, when he resigned to accept a similar charge in the First Church, Germantown. The Choir took the following action on his resignation:

Resolved, That we express our high appreciation of the long and faithful services of Mr. Russell King Miller in our behalf, and of his untiring and successful efforts to elevate the musical standard of our church; and be it further

Resolved, That we extend to him our grateful thanks for the help, the devotion, and the encouragement he has given to us in the past. Our most sincere and earnest wishes for his prosperity and usefulness go with him as he enters upon his new duties.

Mr. William Smith had charge of the organ until the 2d of the following October, on which date Mr. D. E. Crozier, who is still with us, assumed the duties of organist and musical director.

On the 12th of February, 1898, the Choir became a regularly organized body, with Mr. J. Milton Carr as its president, a position he still holds.

Organ Recitals were introduced by Mr.

JOHN MILTON CARR

Miller shortly after the dedication of the new building. At these recitals some of the leading organists of the country have been the performers. The Vesper Services, also introduced by Mr. Miller, and continued by Mr. Crozier, are held during the winter on Sunday afternoons. They are designed to give opportunity for a quiet, restful half-hour to those who feel inclined to enter the church for meditation and prayer. The music, the beauty of the windows, and the holy stillness, all conspire to make lives cleaner, thoughts nobler, and hearts purer.

ORGAN RECITALS AND VESPER SERVICES

On the evening of February 5, 1887, Dr. J. R. Miller invited a number of young ladies to meet at his house to talk over the practicability of an organization in Hollond somewhat similar to the one started the year previous in New York City by Mrs. Bottome, known as the King's Daughters. This was the first meeting of the kind, so far as known, in Philadelphia. It was determined to undertake the work, and the Circle which was then organized was known as the " Ten Times One Club "—the name, " King's Daughters," was soon after adopted. The members of the original circle met together a few times only and then went out by twos to form other

KING'S DAUGHTERS

circles. Many of our young ladies became interested in and subsequently strongly attached to the work. In November, 1892, these circles met together for the first time to form the King's Daughters' Union, the object being "to unite all the King's Daughters of Hollond Church in the endeavor to develop spiritual life and to stimulate to Christian sympathy." Miss Alice Anthony was the first president.

The work performed by this devoted sisterhood has been of inestimable value to the church. The sick in hospitals and in private homes have been visited; old people and little children have been taken to quiet country places; tired and neglected wives and mothers have been given outings; rents have been paid; coal, food, and clothing have been provided for the needy; "shut-ins" have had sympathetic words to brighten their lives, and books and flowers to cheer their loneliness; baskets have been sent to the poor at Christmas times; entertainments have been provided for destitute children; and large contributions have been made to our church building fund. The group of five west windows, and also one or two other windows in the new church, were paid for by the several circles. All honor to these noble workers who thus quietly, unostentatiously, and often self-sacrificingly, con-

A GROUP OF KING'S DAUGHTERS (1898)

tribute to make the hidden current of the church life so full of beauty and so rich in blessing!

The Woman's Home and Foreign Missionary Society was organized about 1882, and has done a noble work in extending MISSIONARY hands of blessing and cheer to SOCIETIES many spiritually destitute portions of our own country and of foreign fields. Mrs. J. R. Miller was the first president. Mrs. R. B. Anthony, who has long been unselfishly devoted to the work, was for ten years its president, an office she was compelled to relinquish on account of ill health. Mrs. W. H. Gill is now the president.

The Society, as originally organized, was an effort to create an interest in foreign mission work, but for a long while past the home and foreign fields have received equal attention— the monthly meetings being alternately devoted to each, when an hour is spent in conference and prayer. The work for foreign fields is largely represented by donations made to schools in Kohlapur, India, and Tokyo, Japan; while the home work is represented by a scholarship in the Mary Gregory School for Indians, Oklahoma Territory. This is known as the Jennie Crosgrave Poulson scholarship, and was established to perpetuate the memory of Mrs. Jennie C. Poulson who was deeply in-

terested not only in the work of the Society
(of which she was treasurer for eleven years),
but also in all the efforts of the church to relieve distress and suffering. Her untimely
death on the 9th of December, 1896, was felt
in many branches of the work.

The Young Ladies' Mission Band was organized in January, 1899, at the request of the
younger members of the church; its object
being to interest girls and young ladies in
foreign mission fields. Miss Alice F. Douglas
was elected president. Its contributions are
given directly to the work of the Woman's
Foreign Missionary Society.

The Boys' and Girls' Mission Band, the object of which is to make its members familiar
with Presbyterian mission stations, was organized in 1886, and has been most helpful in
giving to the children right conceptions of the
importance of missions. Miss Margaret Hunter
(now Mrs. Robert H. Kirk), was the first
president. Miss Minnie Macpherson was its
leader for a number of years.

Suggested by Dr. William M. Paden, and
financially assisted by Mr. Robert C. Ogden,
the Boys' Brigade became one of
BOYS' the organizations of the church
BRIGADE in April, 1895, with a membership of twenty-five. Since that
time it has steadily increased in numbers and

Boys' Brigade (1897)

MAJOR GEORGE A. GOW

proficiency.   It is now one of the leading companies of the city.   George A. Gow was made major, a position he still fills.   It would be a difficult matter to match his faithfulness and devotion.   Not only have the youthful soldiers received training in military movements, but—which is the vital thing in all organizations connected with church work— they have been well taught in other ways. The recitation of Scripture and other devotional exercises, are important features at every drill.   Many boys have been induced to attend Sunday-school, and a number of the members have united with the church.   Miss Minnie I. Taylor has endeared herself to all the boys by her faithful work at the organ.

Every member of the Brigade takes the following pledge:

"I promise and pledge, that so long as I am a member of the Boys' Brigade, I will not use tobacco, nor intoxicating liquor, in any form; that I will not use profane nor vulgar language; that I will obey faithfully the company rules, and that I will at all times set an example of good conduct to my comrades and other boys."

They are taught that Christian gallantry is shown in courage, obedience, helpfulness, and courtesy; that the best soldier is ever the finest, truest gentleman.   The main objects of the movement are : The advancement of Christ's kingdom among boys; the promotion of habits of reverence, discipline, and self-respect; and the cultivation of all that tends towards true Christian manliness.

This institution, which is just across the street from us, is quite as helpful as if it were on our own property and under **SOUTH BRANCH YOUNG MEN'S** our direct control. Many of the **CHRISTIAN** advantages of a great institu-**ASSOCIATION** tional plant are secured through it for Hollond, while other churches have an equal share in its manifold benefits. It ministers to the needs of the body through its gymnasium; of the mind, through its educational classes, libraries, and game rooms; and of the soul, through its religious meetings and spiritual influence. Six members of Hollond are closely identified with its interests—Mr. William L. Cooke, as president; Mr. Frank R. Buckalew, as secretary; and Messrs. Henry A. Walker, James C. Taylor, James D. Blackwood, and William J. Williams as four of the directors.

Many expedients have been employed to inculcate a love for learning and right culture in the hearts of the young people. **LITERARY** Among these have been debating **CIRCLES** clubs for the boys and young men, and reading circles for the young people of both sexes. In recent years,

A LITERARY CIRCLE (1890)

the best known of the latter were the Fifteen Club, which met on Wednesday evenings for the critical study of well-known poets and poems; the Students' Club; and the Chautauqua Circle. The Free Public Library, in the South Branch Young Men's Christian Association building, is proving an important medium of mental culture and information to our people. The University Extension Lectures, in which Dr. Matthew Woods is the recognized leader, are also a valuable source of pleasure and profit.

This is one of the youngest of the working forces, its object being to promote friendship and sociability among the young ATHLETIC people of both sexes, and to give ASSOCIATION them an added opportunity for the cultivation of out-door exercise—such as lawn tennis, croquet, and bicycling. Chess, checker, handball, and quoit clubs have also been formed. By much hard labor, the members transformed the lot back of the new church into a first-class play-ground, and formally dedicated it on the 4th of July, 1896. Dr. Paden and Mr. Ogden made addresses, and the Boys' Brigade was present in full uniform. Many young people enjoy the excellent opportunity thus afforded for physical culture and development.

It has been the policy of the church to

make Christianity as practicable as possible.
Many of the city's poor, who
COAL   would like to be entirely inde-
FUND   pendent, are often obliged to apply to charitable organizations for
fuel in the cold winter months.   In order that
the needy of our congregation may be spared
this humiliation, a branch of the Fuel Savings
Society has been established in the church, and
through it our people are encouraged to de-
posit small amounts at stated periods in the
summer to supply themselves with coal during
the winter.   The money thus collected is placed
in a common fund and coal is purchased at
wholesale rates, enabling the depositors to procure much more for their money than they
otherwise could.   By this means many families have been kept from want and their self-
respect has been maintained.   We find the
plan helpful.

This Society was organized June 28, 1894,
chiefly through the efforts of Mr. Andrew
Martin.   It has become very
BENEFICIAL popular with those careful ones
SOCIETY   who believe in preparing for days
of sickness in time of health.
The Society was a success from the start, and
during these years has been a blessing to many
who have been incapacitated from work
through illness.   The sick benefits are $5

per week, and the sum of $75.00 is, in case of death, paid for funeral expenses. At the end of each fiscal year all the money remaining in the treasury, after the expenses are paid, is divided *pro rata* among the members in good standing. The Society is then re-organized for the ensuing year.

This Association, known as the "Samuel M. Kennedy," issued its first stock on the 10th of September, 1894. Mr. James C. Taylor, who was at the heart of the movement, became its first president. It has had a very successful career. Many of our people are stockholders and therefore directly interested in its well-being. It is proving a good investment to those who are using it merely as a savings fund, as it has paid an annual profit of over six per cent. It is also helpful to those who through it have bought and are now paying for their homes. In encouraging many to cultivate habits of thrift and economy it has been of very practical service.

BUILDING ASSOCIATION

It is a good thing for churches to have their workers come together now and then to learn what the several organizations are trying to accomplish. For several years this has been very successfully carried out in Hollond. The plan is thus de-

CONFERENCE OF WORKERS

scribed in *The Open Church* of April, 1897:

" The various organizations working in the church are all brought together in an annual conference of Hollond workers. They gather at a tea, prepared by a committee of ladies, and then every department is represented by some chosen speaker. This is an original idea, or at least carried out in an original way, and it has been found to work very admirably. The pastors present the work from their point of view, the superintendents of the Sunday-school voice its needs, and each department is represented through an appointed speaker." Thus all are made familiar with what is being attempted.

The Christian Endeavor Society was organized in the chapel parlor on the 4th of October, 1892, with the following members: Rev. W. M. Paden, D. D., Rev. J. R. Miller, D. D., Mrs. M. H. Allen, Miss Katheryn T. Anderson, Joseph Anderson, Thomas Boyle, Miss Margaret Burns, J. Milton Carr, G. Rhea Carr, Ray H. Carter, Miss Lotta M. Cavin, Charles A. Chew, Miss Jessie S. Connerd, Miss Jennie Crosgrave, Miss Helen Crossley, Miss Caroline A. Douglas, Miss Alice F. Douglas, Miss Margaret Eddie, Miss Sara Eddie, Miss Sadie Fleming, Harry P. Ford, Cleveland Frame, Miss Sara J.

Hanna, Miss Martha Hartman, Charles A. Hoehling, Miss Mary R. Hunter, Miss Katherine Hunter, Miss Jessie Jamieson, George H. Kelly, Samuel M. Kennedy, Miss Emma Knous, Joseph MacMorris, Miss Minnie Macpherson, Miss Margaret Macpherson, Miss Tillie McKinley, John McKnight, Miss Rebecca McNevin, John Molitor, Miss Lizzie Orr, Miss Maggie Patton, Miss Lillie Pairman, George M. Peak, Miss C. E. Ramsay, Miss Malvina Toram, Miss Clara A. Walker, Miss Lillie Williamson, Miss Etta Wilson.

The following united as associated members : Miss Helen Gillison, Walter Higgenbotham, William K. Miller, Donald Pairman, Miss Hattie Ramsay, Miss Nettie Reid.

This movement was the outgrowth of a flourishing Young People's Association, which, since 1876, had been an important factor in the advancement of the general work. Under the able leadership of Mr. George H. Kelly, the first president, the new organization was a success from the beginning. So many active workers are now connected with it that, with the exception of the monthly consecration service, which is usually under the care of the president, it is seldom that a member, however prominent, is called on to lead more than one meeting during the year. It has frequently happened at the monthly roll-call that all the members, save perhaps a half-dozen, have responded to their names by a verse, a prayer, or a brief talk; once only *one* failed to respond. It has been a long time since any of the members have responded to their names by answering " Present," and we trust that such a questionable method of easing one's conscience will never again be revived.

The names of the leaders for the entire year, and notes relative to the local work, are printed and then inserted in the Presbyterian Handbook, which is issued annually. By having this useful booklet constantly at hand, the members become familiar with the work that is being carried on by the Presbyterian Church through its several Boards. As a rule, much is made of the annual meeting in October, at which time the interior of the chapel is decorated, a good supper enjoyed, reports made by the chairmen of the several committees, and new officers elected.

Much of the far-reaching usefulness of this important organization is doubtless due to the fact that a fairly successful effort is constantly being made to have *all* the members interested in the work. Every member is on a committee, and is expected to help. The several committees touch life at many points, and open to the young people neglected fields of untold usefulness. Many missions in our own and other lands have been encouraged by substantial tokens of remembrance from the Missionary Committee ; sailors on many seas, and the sick in many of our hospitals, have been made better by helpful books, magazines, and tracts which have been distributed by the Good Literature Committee ; and the entire membership has grown into larger usefulness through the impelling influence of these and the other committees in inspiring in them a desire to be helpful to others. It is but just that special mention should be made of the faithful work of the Floating Committee, which holds a meeting every Sunday morning at the Barracks at League Island; assists the chaplain (by leading the singing) at the service held an hour later on the receiving ship Richmond; conducts an Endeavor service on the Richmond every Wednesday evening; and frequently visits the Marine Hospital. Much of the success of the recent work has been due to the enthusiastic leadership of Miss Sara Eddie. Letters of grateful appreciation from soldiers in Manila and Cuba, and from sailors on men-of-war, speak volumes in favor of the value of the work. Rev. Thomas A. Gill, chaplain in the U. S. Navy, and for a long while stationed at League Island, thus wrote to Miss Eddie after his recent removal to another station :

" I can hardly tell you what a solace and

comfort the co-operation of yourself and co-workers was to me in my work on the Richmond at League Island. Aside from the bearing of it on the common Christian work, in which we were all interested, it greatly encouraged and sustained me personally in the isolation attending such work as mine on a ship-of-war. Your faithful presence and co-working made me feel that I was in touch with the real, warm Christian world. I pointedly indicated the value of your co-operation in my report to the Secretary of the Navy at the close of last year. I indeed miss your help on the ship where I now am."

Two handsome pictures—"Christ in Gethsemane," and the battleship "Brooklyn"—the former from Chaplain Gill and the latter from the men of the "Brooklyn," have been presented to our workers as a mark of appreciation. These pictures hang on the wall of the chapel parlor and are highly prized.

At the annual meeting in October of this year (1899), Miss Sara Eddie was elected president; Miss Sallie Peak and Mr. James H. Taitt, vice-presidents; Mr. W. C. M. Barstler, recording secretary; Miss Josephine Bloch, treasurer; and Miss Sara F. Barstler, corresponding secretary.

After several conferences of the Executive

ISS SARA EDDIE

Committee of the Christian Endeavor Society, it was resolved, with the approval **THE JUNIOR CHRISTIAN ENDEAVOR SOCIETY** of the pastors, to organize a Junior Endeavor Society. This interesting event took place on the 29th of March, 1896, and James D. Gerhardt was elected president. The original members were Roscoe C. Barstler, William E. Batchelder, Eva Begley, Katie Bentz, Lillie Bickley, Ida Caldwell, Nellie Caldwell, Frank Christopher, Crete Connelly, Lillie Dobbins, Maud Dobbins, Orpha Farren, Emma G. Gardiner, James D. Gerhardt, Robert A. L. Hampton, Robert J. Hunter, George W. Johnston, Maidie Kennedy, Wilson Kessler, Bella Kyle, Cassie Little, Walter Martin, Hattie McKinley, Vinnie Mintzer, Lizzie Morrison, Albert A. Myers, Louis O'Donnell, Louise C. Roelofs, Lizzie Taitt, Samuel J. Taitt, Florence Thorp, Mary Torrens, Bessie Selfridge, Charles A. Smith, Raymond Steinbach, Walter G. Steinbach, Anna Stewart, Mamie Stewart, and John Stinson.

The children have had many pleasant outings. On one of the excursions to Menlo Park, given by the Sunday-school, they had a special car to themselves. When Dr. Paden left for Utah, the Juniors made him a present of a fountain pen '' as a slight token of their appreciation of his loving-kindness to them and of

their affectionate regard for him." They also
gave him a five-dollar gold piece, with the following note :

"We understand that you are going to a
field scarcely larger than Hollond was when
you came here fourteen years ago. Our parents tell us that you had not been with us long
before you began to feel, and to make them
feel, the need of a new church, and that you
gave yourself and them but little rest until our
beautiful new building crowned your efforts
with success. Now we have been thinking
that you will not be in Salt Lake City very
long before both you and your people there
will be feeling something of the same need of
a new place of worship, so we have determined
to give you Five Dollars to start a Building
Fund *at once*. You will find the amount in a
coin of pure gold—emblematic of the love we
bear you. If you need more money let us
know and we will see you through."

To this Dr. Paden made the following response :

"No token of hope or love which I have
ever received has pleased me more than yours;
it was so full of confidence in the good things
to come. The pen I shall use every day; if I
do not learn to write more plainly, I think I
shall at least write the more hopefully and lovingly because of your gift; and the gold is

A GROUP OF HOLLOND JUNIORS (1896)

A GROUP OF HOLLOND JUNIORS (1896)

worth more to me than a large nugget from the Klondike. I hope you will one day know that it has increased ten thousand fold."

Under the loving care of Miss Sara Barstler and Miss Margaret Burns, the work is still carried on with every promise of much future usefulness to the church and school.

The two photographs of the members, which are here reproduced, were taken on the first excursion to Bartram's Gardens, May 16, 1896.

The Ushers' Association is one of the youngest and most progressive of our many activities. It was organized on USHERS' the 16th of October, 1893, and ASSOCIATION rapidly developed into one of the most useful of our working forces. In seating and making comfortable the congregation, in the quiet and reverent methods of taking the collection, in the maintenance of order, and in the welcome extended to visitors, its members are constantly exercising a blessed and beneficent influence. They are also responsible for the editorial and financial management of the church paper, *The Hollond Reminder;* they see to it that it is issued regularly, free of expense to the church treasury.

At the great Peace Jubilee in the fall of 1898, one of the handsomest stands on Broad street was erected by the Ushers in front of the church, from which they realized a total sum of $696.00, the net profits being $357.00. This amount is being used to assist in meeting the expense incurred in the publication of *The Reminder*.

At the monthly meetings of the organization routine business is transacted, interesting papers are read, instructive debates on live questions are indulged in, and able addresses are delivered.

The group of members which is here reproduced was photographed January 1, 1897.

On the back row, at the extreme left of the picture, is George H. Kelly, the first president; then follow in order William B. Hens, Charles A. Hoehling, William R. Taitt, James W. Stevenson, James C. Taylor, H. P. Ford, Charles A. Chew, Charles Hunter, Joseph Mac-Morris, William A. Leonard, Andrew Martin, and Andrew R. Poulson.

On the middle row, beginning at the left, are Daniel J. Weaver, Harry B. Smithson, John Russell, Frank L. Hansen, and William E. Thompson.

On the lower row, beginning at the left, are Joseph C. Ramsey, Eugene Smith, Huntley Murdock, George Rhea Carr, T. Ellwood Frame, and Chester D. Griesemer.

In the death of Mr. William R. Taitt, on the 28th of March, 1899, at the early age of thirty

USHERS' ASSOCIATION (1897)

years, the Association met with its greatest loss. At the time of his death he was the president of the organization. By his quiet influence, remarkable energy and unselfish devotion he had done much to increase its prosperity and usefulness. Mr. Charles Traub succeeded him in the presidency.

The following is copied from a book recently issued by Dodd, Mead & Co., New York, entitled " Modern Methods in Church Work ":

" The ushers at one end of the church are as important as the minister at the other. The first impression which strangers receive on coming into a church is usually from the ushers. The courteous welcome and ready attention, and the prompt seating of visitors, as well as the regular attendants, when necessary, is no small factor in the success of winning people.

" If there is any body of men who need to be prayed for, who ought to pray for themselves, that they may at once realize the importance, delicacy and dignity of their office, it is the ushers of a church.

" The Ushers' Association of the Hollond Memorial Church, Philadelphia, is deserving of mention. This organization has published in a neat attractive form its constitution and by-laws, together with the names of the officers and members. The suggestions to ushers contained in this booklet are so capital that a copy of them should be in the hands of every usher in the country :

1. Be at your post fifteen minutes before time for service.

2. Be careful to reserve seats when requested to do so.

3. Fill your front seats first.

4. Know how many each pew will seat, and see that it is filled when the house is crowded.

5. Make an effort to seat friends together.

6. Give strangers the best seats, and see that they have a hymn-book or programme. (Read Hebrews xiii : 2.)

7. The head usher should make it his business to direct the ushering. He should see that the house is evenly seated, and that the ushers do their work properly.

8. Never seat anyone during prayer or the rendering of special music.

9. Be prompt in starting the collection, but go slow in taking it, and be careful not to slight any one.

10. Keep the air good. If it becomes close, open windows during the singing.

11. Be quiet and reverent in your work.

12. Do not permit groups to assemble in the back part of the church and talk before or during the service.

" Once a year this Society gives a supper and entertainment to the men of the church.

CHARLES TRAUB

The work of the Association is then reviewed, other short addresses are made, and a general good time is realized. In speaking of this Association, the Rev. J. R. Miller, D. D., says : ' It has worked admirably. It is a good thing for the young men themselves. It has trained them to thoughtfulness and helpfulness in many ways. They have learned to greet people cordially and to take an interest in strangers, old people, and poor people. Beside, it has been of great advantage to the church, assuring system and order in the seating of people, and in the taking up of collections.' ''

The present membership is as follows : Dr. George E. Martin, Rev. L. L. Overman, Furman Algie, Royal Balch, Samuel H. Barstler, W. C. M. Barstler, Thomas Boyle, Frank R. Buckalew, Carroll H. Burton, W. S. Butler, Robert Carnswarth, J. Milton Carr, G. Rhea Carr, Charles A. Chew, W. L. Cooke, M. G. Crillman, William Cutler, Frank J. Day, Warren P. Dexter, John Dunn, George Flanagan, H. P. Ford, T. Ellwood Frame, Wm. H. Fulmer, William K. Gorham, George A. Gow, Chester Griesemer, Frank L. Hansen, Lewis P. Harding, John C. Heil, Wm. B. Hens, Hermann Hillebrand, Frank Hitchens, Chas. A. Hoehling, Charles Hunter, George H. Kelly, Wm. A. Leonard, Harry Light, T. H. Loder, George Loder, Benjamin F. Lutton,

Joseph MacMorris, Andrew Martin, Huntley R. Murdock, David McAfee, Daniel B. McAllister, William McFarland, George D. McIlvaine, Thomas L. Niven, Chas. Oelschalger, Hugh O'Neill, George M. Peak, R. H. Preston, Andrew R. Poulson, J. C. Ramsey, J. H. Restine, John Russell, Harry P. Smithson, J. W. Stevenson, Robert J. Sterritt, James H. Taitt, James C. Taylor, Wm. E. Thompson, Wm. J. Tomlinson, Charles Traub, J. S. Tweddle, Henry A. Walker, James Wallace, Daniel J. Weaver, J. E. Williams, David Woods.

For many years this helpful gathering for conference and prayer was held on Friday evenings ; on the 23rd of November, 1898, the meeting night was changed to Wednesday. While these services are never so largely attended as they should be, yet those who come find them helpful and stimulating. With but few exceptions, those who are doing the most to advance the interests of the church are to be found at one or both of our week-night prayer meetings, and it is doubtless here that they get much of the spiritual stimulus for continuance in well-doing. The value of these quiet gatherings to our church, and to those who regularly attend them, cannot be overestimated. Miss Katie Linsenmeyer has long been the faithful organist.

CONGREGA-
TIONAL
PRAYER
MEETING

The money devoted to this purpose is economically administered. Fortunately, there are but few desperately poor people connected with our church, and that this is so is doubtless due largely to our policy to give as little financial aid as possible, but rather to encourage and help the needy to be self-supporting and self-reliant. In the carrying out of this policy many families to-day are living in comfort who in all probability would otherwise be helpless. We give financial assistance only when it seems to be absolutely necessary; and those to whom money is given are encouraged to return it, if possible, in order that it may continue its helpful mission to others. Our aim is to build up character, even in our charities.

DEACONS' FUND

This helpful Class was organized by Dr. Martin in January, 1899, and meets on Friday evening. The course of study covers three years—the first, to be devoted to the authorship, main divisions, purpose, and dates of the books of the Old Testament; the second, to a similar study of the books of the New Testament; and the third, to teaching in the Sunday-school and pursuing a course of reading directed by Dr. Martin. The conditions of membership in this Class are: 1st, a pur-

NORMAL CLASS

pose to complete the course in three years;
and, 2nd, an earnest desire to know more of
God's Word. From its very nature the work
has promise of much future usefulness and is
already very popular with its members.

From the dedication of the chapel down to
the present time a number of papers have
been issued to keep the work of
CHURCH   the church before the congrega-
PAPERS   tion. The first paper was published in October, 1874. It was
a small four-paged monthly, and was known
as *Our Leaflet*. It printed but little local
news. The November *Leaflet* contained a list
of the officers and teachers of the school. Un-
fortunately, however, the last names only of
the workers were given. Obeying a well-
known law of nature, the *Leaflet* appears to
have passed out of existence before the snows
of December came.

In January, 1875, *Our Sabbath-School Helper*,
a much larger paper, was issued. Of its twelve
columns but one was devoted to the happen-
ings of Hollond. Two or three numbers only
were published.

The successor of the *Helper* was *The Hollond
Quarterly*, which appeared in September, 1879.
Most of the space was devoted to orders of review exercise. The last number appears to
have been issued in December, 1880.

In November, 1882, *The Hollond Monthly* made its first appearance, with Dr. Miller and Mr. W. L. Cooke as editors, and Mr. H. A. Walker as business manager. It was published under the supervision of the Young People's Pastor's Aid Association. The first page was devoted to stories, the second and third to church and school matters, and the last to advertisements. The advertisements were discontinued with the February, 1883, issue. After March, 1883, the paper was not published until December of the same year, when it awoke to renewed activity under the editorial management of Dr. Paden and Messrs. R. C. Ogden, W. L. Cooke, Charles A. Oliver, and Samuel M. Kennedy. Mr. H. A. Walker retained his position as business manager, with Mr. Chas. A. Chew as treasurer. In the February number appeared Mr. MacMorris's excellent cut of the chapel, which has become so familiar to us. The paper appeared monthly up to and including January, 1885, and then in March, June and November, 1885, and in January, February, March, May, and June, 1886.

The Hollond Quarterly was issued in November, 1886, and was almost the exact counterpart of the *Monthly*. Drs. Paden and Miller, and Messrs. R. C. Ogden, W. L. Cooke, Samuel Semple, and S. M. Kennedy were the editors.

The Hollond Messenger, issued January,

1888, was the next paper. But three numbers appear to have been published, the last one being in December, 1888. It was larger and more interesting than any of its predecessors. The first three pages were devoted to church news, and the fourth to advertisements.

In the spring of 1892, Mr. Robert C. Ogden, at a teachers' meeting, spoke of the importance of a church paper and suggested that one be published. The outcome of this suggestion was *The Hollond Reminder*, which made its initial appearance on June 5th of that year. It contained no advertisements and all the expenses of publication were paid by Mr. Ogden. After continuing as a *weekly* for nineteen consecutive numbers (the last number bearing date of October 9th, 1892), it was changed to a *monthly*—the first number of which was published in November, 1892. As a monthly, it was published by the Church Press Association, which allowed the church the first eight pages, free, for local news, the Association having the privilege of using the other eight pages for advertising purposes. This arrangement continued for four years, when the contract was canceled with the October, 1896, issue, in order that the church might undertake the publication of the paper on its own responsibility. Under the new arrangement, the paper was published by the Christian

D. B. McALLISTER

Endeavor Society, the first number appearing in December, 1896, with Mr. Chester Griesemer as the business manager. The paper contained sixteen pages in addition to the cover, and presented an attractive appearance, a special cover design having been drawn for it by Miss Caroline A. Douglas.

Owing to Mr. Griesemer's serious illness, the business control of the paper was offered to and accepted by the Ushers' Association, and Mr. Ellwood Frame was appointed business manager. The first number under the new management appeared in April, 1897. After rendering valuable service, Mr. Frame resigned, and Mr. Daniel B. McAllister succeeded to his position. Although very much engaged with his personal business, Mr. McAllister has given much time to this labor of love ; and it has been largely due to his earnest efforts, ably seconded by Mr. Thomas L. Niven, that *The Reminder* has been continued to the present time. It is pleasant to state, that since its first appearance in June, 1892, the paper has been published without missing a single issue, save that of November, 1896, which was due to changing publishers.

Bound copies of *The Reminder* may be found in the church library, and also in the library of the Presbyterian Historical Society. H. P. Ford has edited the paper from its beginning.

BIOGRAPHICAL SKETCHES

"Our echoes roll from soul to soul,
And grow forever and forever."

One cannot make even a general review of the history of Hollond without being impressed with the vigorous and uplifting nature of the work, and with the singular devotion of the workers—characteristics which have marked the undertaking from the very beginning. In the early years, men and women of culture and refinement, who could lend an added grace to any position, left a pleasant church home, with delightful spiritual and social surroundings, to give themselves with consecrated energy to the cause of the poor and the friendless in a neglected portion of the city ; and not for a brief season only, but for long years of faithful service. Not only were they directly helpful at the time but their influence has continued through the years, and the Hollond life of to-day is cast in a finer mould because of them. To notice with any degree of fullness all who deserve special mention would require volumes; we must be content with brief sketches of a few of the official leaders.

Henry Augustus Boardman, D. D., was born in Troy, New York, January 9th, 1808, and was graduated from Yale College, **HENRY A. BOARDMAN, D. D.** in September, 1829, being the valedictorian of his class. He studied law for a year and then determined to devote his life to the work of the gospel ministry. In the fall of 1830 he entered Princeton Theological Seminary, from which he was graduated three years later. He preached his first sermons in the Tenth Church July 28th, 1833, from the texts Luke 6: 43–45; Isaiah 1: 2, 3. At a congregational meeting held on the 2nd of the following September he received a call to become the pastor. This he accepted and on the 8th day of November he was ordained and installed. This was his first and only charge, and for forty-three years he filled the pulpit " with distinguished ability, learning and fidelity."

In 1853, Dr. Boardman was elected by the General Assembly to the chair of Pastoral Theology in Princeton Seminary, made vacant by the death of Archibald Alexander, which he declined to accept—many of the leading citizens, irrespective of denominational affiliation, uniting with the members of his own congregation in urging him to remain in Philadelphia. In 1854, he was elected moderator of the (O. S.) General Assembly.

On the 5th of May, 1876, Dr. Boardman addressed a tender and affectionate letter to his people, requesting them, in view of his impaired health, to unite with him in an application to Presbytery dissolving the pastoral relationship. In this letter he thus generously alludes to his two associates : '' Restricted of late years to one sermon a Sabbath, my lack of service has been liberally supplied by my able and excellent associates, the Rev. Louis R. Fox, from January, 1872, to June, 1874, and since November 29th, 1874, by the Rev. J. Henry Sharpe. On the occasion of Mr. Fox's resignation, speaking not less for me than for yourselves, you bore your cordial and united testimony to ' his piety and earnestness, his fidelity and zeal, in the discharge of his co-pastoral duties.' And you will pay the same tribute to his successor, Mr. Sharpe, from whose lips (let me add) I have never heard, in the eighteen months he has been with us, a single common-place sermon. My intercourse with these brethren has been of the most refreshing character. In serving you faithfully, their uniform courtesy and kindness towards myself have converted this very delicate relation into a source of the greatest comfort and encouragement.''

Very reluctantly the congregation determined to acquiesce in Dr. Boardman's request. At a

REV. H. A. BOARDMAN, D. D.

meeting of Presbytery held in the Tenth Presbyterian Church an the 25th of May, 1876, the following action was taken on the resignation :

" Resolved, That the Presbytery accede to the united request of Dr. Boardman and the Tenth Church for the dissolution of the pastoral relation."

Resolutions of regret and esteem were adopted by both the Presbytery and the church. By the vote of both bodies Dr. Boardman was made " pastor emeritus," a position he held until his death on the 15th of June, 1880, in his seventy-third year. He had returned the preceding day from Atlantic City, and although he was known to be ill his sickness caused no serious alarm. He grew worse, however, during the night and quietly passed away the following morning.

Dr. Boardman was an able writer. His printed works embrace above a dozen volumes and some twenty-five or thirty discourses and other pamphlets. Of his ability as a preacher, Dr. Alfred Nevin wrote : " He was evangelical and elevated in his thought, and pure, simple, and direct in his style. He charmed while he instructed his people, and he bound them to him by the ties of reverential love. He was uncompromisingly orthodox in his doctrinal beliefs ; always and everywhere he maintained his Presbyterian opinion." Dr. William P. Breed said of him, "For ability and true manly dignity, for fidelity to sound doctrine, for richness of pulpit instruction, for purity and felicity of literary style, for persuasive eloquence, and for reach of healthful influence, he left nothing to be desired."

The first sermon preached in the Hollond Chapel was by Dr. Boardman. He was interested in all that pertained to its welfare. Mr. Charles E. Morris bore this generous testimony : "When the books shall be opened, and every secret thing be made known, it will be found that to Dr. Boardman, more than to any other human agency, has the success and present prosperity of our Mission [Hollond] been due."

On one of the visits of Dr. A. P. Happer to this country from China, he and Dr. Rice were dining with Dr. Boardman. The theme of conversation was the subject in which the three were so deeply interested—the Moyamensing Mission. Turning to Dr. Happer, Dr. Boardman said :

"*Some day you will come from China on a visit to your native country, as now, and you will find the Tenth Church Mission not in its present cramped quarters on Carpenter street, but in a large, magnificent, well-furnished cathedral church, equal, or even superior, in its equipments for aggressive work, to the mother church.*"

This prophecy of Dr. Boardman has had remarkable fulfillment.

Rev. Dr. A. P. Happer, at the age of twenty-four, became the first superintendent of the old Moyamensing Mission school. In **REV. ANDREW** 1893, he wrote Dr. Paden as fol- **P. HAPPER,** **D.D., M.D.** lows: "In November, 1842, at the request of the teachers, I commenced the duties of superintendent of the Moyamensing Mission." In view of his early association with our work, it has been thought well to give a somewhat extended account of his life. The following abbreviated article, from the pen of William Rankin, Esq., was taken from the January, 1895, *Church at Home and Abroad :*

Andrew Patton Happer was born in Monongahela City, Pa., October 20, 1818, and died in Wooster, Ohio, October 27, 1894.

Dr. Happer, then a graduate of Jefferson College, having completed his theological course at Allegheny, was studying medicine in Philadelphia, where he took the degree of M.D. in the University of Pennsylvania. In 1844, he was ordained by the Presbytery of Ohio, and on the 22d of June, that year, sailed from New York for Canton.

The mission having succeeded in entering and establishing itself in Canton, Dr. Happer, on the 11th of November, 1847, married Elizabeth, daughter of Rev. Dyer Ball, of the American Board, who became the mother of his four daughters, who, under the appointment of the Presbyterian Board, were at times his co-laborers in the field; also his son, who ministered to him in his last hours.

Mrs. Happer's health gave way in 1854, making a change necessary. Dr. Happer embarked with his family for the United States in December of that year. He returned to the field in 1859, and in 1862 the first Presbyterian church was organized, with seven native members. He became its pastor and gathered into that fold some five hundred converts. He detached members as colonies to form nine other churches.

In December, 1865, Mrs. Elizabeth Happer departed this life. A suitable provision for his motherless children required that the father should bring them to America. In October, 1869, he returned to China, having on the 6th of that month married Miss A. L. Elliott, who, for twenty years, had been a teacher in Western Pennsylvania. She died four years later.

Dr. Happer's third marriage was on March 18, 1875, to Miss Hannah J. Shaw, a member of the mission, who survives him.

It was not until after fourteen years of continuous labor that he consented to another furlough. He came home, but not to rest.

The project of a Chinese Christian college, permanently endowed, engaged his attention. He came to New York, and for several weeks was engaged in securing the desired funds. Success crowned his efforts, and over $100 000 were placed in the hands of trustees in New York. The Chinese College was inaugurated on paper and he was made the first president. Mrs. Happer went back with her husband to China. For two years they labored together. Mrs. Happer's health now failed, compelling her return home. Her husband followed a few months later, mainly from the same cause, resigning the presidency of the college to its trustees. They removed to Wooster, whence the great soul of this busy man entered into the joy of his Lord.

Mr. Wurts was born in Louisville, Kentucky, August 31, 1820, and died in Philadelphia December 15, 1881. He removed to this city in his youth and at an early age became a member of the Tenth Presbyterian Church.

MAURICE A. WURTS

He took an active interest in many branches of the work of that church but was specially devoted to mission labors in the neglected portions of the city.

In 1847, he became the superintendent of the Moyamensing Mission, which then met in the second story of the Native American Hose

Company house on Carpenter street, below Tenth. The following year he succeeded in having erected a comfortable Sunday-school building and through the impetus thus given to the work, together with his able leadership, the membership of the school grew from fifty to above four hundred. His strong personality, love for children, devotion to the work, and deep spiritual earnestness, admirably fitted him for the responsible position which he continued to fill with ever-increasing usefulness for eleven years.

In 1858, he removed to West Philadelphia and became the superintendent of the Greenway Mission, which has since been organized into the Greenway Presbyterian Church. To this work he gave seven years of faithful and successful service.

Mr. Wurts was twice superintendent of the Sunday-school of the Tenth Church. He was one of the first elders of the Woodland Presbyterian Church.

"His enthusiasm and unselfish devotion to Sunday-school mission work led to his appointment as secretary of Missions of the American Sunday-School Union, and recording secretary of its Board, February 19, 1861," a position he continued to fill with great acceptance until his death in 1881, a period of twenty years. A booklet entitled "An Unselfish Life," set-

MAURICE A. WURTS

ting forth the value of his work to the Sunday-School Union and other religious enterprises, was published shortly after his death.

Strong leaders have been connected with our work from the beginning and Mr. Wurts was among the foremost of them. He was largely instrumental in laying the firm foundation upon which much of the subsequent success of the Hollond school has been built. A lady who was a teacher during his superintendency thus writes of his work and its results:

"I was not with Mr. Wurts in the early years of his work in Moyamensing. but I have often heard him speak of the difficulties encountered, the rough surroundings, and the unsatisfactory arrangements in the old hose-house, with boards placed on boxes or barrels for seats, and the rough, undisciplined element he had to contend with.

"It was his aim to make this a model school; but with the raw material he had to work with, this involved much patient and persevering work.

"When I entered the school I was given a class of fourteen girls. With the exception of two or three, they were utterly untrained, unkempt little waifs, picked up from the neighborhood. Often bare feet and bare heads presented themselves in the class, heads evidently not under the subduing influences of comb or brush; faces and hands free from any sense of the need of soap and water. We began with requiring cleanliness, hoping that the next grace might be induced to follow. After a few years the effect on the school became so manifest that at our regular church anniversaries, our dear pastor, Dr. Boardman, looking over the two schools brought together in the Tenth Church, would often remark that a stranger would not be able to tell which was the church school and which the mission.

'' The change in the neighborhood was also quite as marked. When I first took a class, it was considered unsafe for the lady teachers to go alone, and as Mr. Wurts was very desirous that each family should be visited, it required no little courage to carry out his wishes. Drunken men, most untidy houses, and occasional fights with brickbats, etc., were encountered, but it was not so very long before all this was changed, and a great improvement seen in the character and appearance of the neighborhood.''

Dr. Rice was born April 30th, 1817, at Lowville, New York. He was graduated from Wesleyan University, Middletown, Connecticut, in 1837. He was tutor in languages in that University from the time of his graduation until 1840, when he became the

WILLARD
MARTIN RICE
D. D.

REV. W. M. RICE, D. D. (1896)

principal of a classical school in Philadelphia—
a position he continued to hold until 1856,
when he assumed charge of the Moyamensing
Mission of the Tenth Presbyterian Church.
Two years later, the Mission developed into
the Moyamensing Presbyterian Church, and
Dr. Rice became the first pastor.   He remained
in charge until 1863, when he resigned to become the pastor of the Fourth Presbyterian
Church, where he stayed until 1874 ; in that
year he received and accepted a call from
Trinity Church, Berwyn, Pa., where he remained until 1876.

The following action was taken by the
congregation of the Moyamensing Church, October, 14th, 1863, on the resignation of Dr.
Rice :

"Resolved, That in uniting with Mr. Rice
in his request, we do so with a deep sense of
his faithful labors and patient sacrifices in our
behalf.

"Resolved, That in the harmony and love
which should ever exist between pastor and
people, there is not a single link wanting in
this whole church.

"Resolved, That during the five years of his
pastorate, his untiring zeal and faithful ministrations have endeared him to us by constantly increasing ties, and bound us together
by a love and harmony which we can never
cease to remember with gratitude.

"Resolved, That we unite in prayer to the

Great Head of the Church in behalf of our pastor that his useful life may be spared ; that wherever his lot may be cast he may win the same love which we here desire to express towards him, and that he, who has all his servants in his keeping, would graciously watch over him and his, and make him eminently useful in his Church.''

Dr. Rice was a member of the Board of Publication from 1860 to 1887. Since 1862 he has been its recording clerk. He has also been engaged in much literary work in connection with the Board.

He has been clerk of the Presbytery of Philadelphia since 1858, with the exception of the years 1874-1877, during which time he was a member of the Presbytery of Chester. He was clerk of the Synod of Philadelphia from 1868 to 1882, and has frequently been a member of the General Assembly. He received his degree of D. D. from his Alma Mater in 1866.

On the 7th of July, 1840, Dr. Rice married Miss Elizabeth McDowell, daughter of the Rev. John McDowell, D. D., for sixty years one of the most prominent clergymen of the Presbyterian Church.

Although he has reached an advanced age, he gives daily attention to business in his office in the Witherspoon Building. His mental faculties are unimpared and he retains much of his physical vigor. He is one of our finest Latin, Greek, and Hebrew scholars and retains his knowledge of these languages to a wonderful degree. His knowledge on all matters relating to the history of the Presbyterian Church in Philadelphia is almost encyclopedic. He is deeply interested in all that pertains to Hollond.

The question has frequently been asked, " How did the Hollond Church get its name? "

HARRIET HOLLOND It was so called in memory of Harriet Hollond, a member of the Tenth Church, who gave $10,000 towards the erection of the chapel at Federal and Clarion streets, which we now use for our Sunday-school and prayer-meeting services. The following excerpts were kindly made by Mr. William L. DuBois, from a memorial volume written by Dr. Henry A. Boardman :

Miss Harriet Hollond was born October 12, 1812, and was the daughter of Charles and Ann E. Hollond. Of her father it is said, " he was an English gentlemen of honorable descent whose generous culture and attractive qualities lent grace and dignity to the sterling virtues which formed the base of his character." He died in March, 1831, leaving a widow and five children, Harriet being the oldest, although she outlived them all. Her mother and two sisters, dying within a short time of each other, left her alone in the world so far as family was concerned. This heavy stroke fell with great severity, and her slender frame seemed as though it must sink under its accumulated burdens. Her flesh and strength declined. In 1847 her physicians prescribed a visit to Europe, and in company with Dr. H. A. Boardman and family, she spent thirteen months abroad and there is no doubt that, under Providence, this was the chief means of prolonging her valuable life for many years.

Her chief characteristics were Humility and Benevolence. One who knew her well for forty years said, " I have never known in any sphere of life, a more humble Christian, and never a more benevolent one." She had inherited a generous fortune, and her beautiful home at 1214 Walnut street was furnished with articles of taste and handiwork. Many curios she had collected in Europe, while many were keepsakes of her friends, but there was no extravagance or ostentation ; her controlling reason for having these things lay in the gratification they afforded her friends.

She had as much of that homely Saxon quality we call common sense, next to piety the most valuable of all endowments, as often falls to the lot of man or woman.

In 1855, upon the death of her attached

HARRIET HOLLOND

friend, Mrs. Ellen W. Jones, she was made
superintendent of the Female Sabbath-school
of the Tenth Church, a position never better
filled by anyone, and in which she continued
until the time of her death. Nothing but
sickness or absence from the city could keep
her from her post. Always punctual, familiar
with the details of every class, knowing even
every scholar by name, she recognized at a
glance the exigencies of each session, occa-
sioned by absence and other causes, and with
a happy facility provided for them. The last
ten of these years were dedicated to the school
under circumstances which most persons would
have regarded as a sufficient reason for declin-
ing active service. A severe illness in 1859 at
Newport revealed an organic disease of the
heart. This caused her to be an invalid for the
rest of her life, and to suffer numerous attacks
from this malady ; but even then she spared
herself no labor that might contribute to the
well being of the Sunday-school.

To the work of the Missionary Society of
the Tenth Church Miss Hollond gave her utmost sympathies, her unwearied care and her
munificent benefactions. She was not the
official head of the Society. It had no such
head. No one cared to be '' president,'' and
she would not consent to be. She was the
treasurer—a treasurer who, after spending the

inadequate contributions received from the congregation, uniformly supplied all deficiences from her own purse.

Her benevolent sympathies demanded yet wider scope. In the winter of 1857-1858, Winthrop Sargent, one of the elders of the Tenth Church, with the aid of his brethren, commenced a meeting for social prayer. The encouragement given it was so great that two years later (March, 1860) Miss Hollond rented a suitable house on South Juniper street, and a lady well qualified for the task was employed to superintend operations. Here the women, to the number of sixty or seventy, would meet on certain evenings to receive religious instructions, and to sew—making clothing for the missionaries. The ample stock of materials demanded by the formidable corps of workers being supplied by Miss Hollond. Besides, there was a "sewing school" for the young, on Saturday afternoons, the children not only sewing for the missionaries, but cheerfully contributing their pennies to buy libraries for the missionary children. Sunday afternoons, at two o'clock, there was an adult Bible class, and Sunday evenings were given to a religious service, conducted by Mr. Sargent, mentioned above, and a few excellent brethren. Christmas holidays were always remembered, and the clothing prepared for the missionary boxes was displayed at that time. In the evening, after a brief religious exercise, all repaired to the parlor, where a bountiful table was spread, and where Miss Hollond, with the few young ladies she had invited to help her, took pleasure in passing the refreshments with her own hands, addressing a word or two to each by name, and putting up special parcels for their invalids at home. Of course the children were remembered, and had their festival on one of the holiday afternoons.

While she was specially interested in missionary work, she was one of the largest contributors in the city to the several Boards of the Church, and the other objects which make their annual appeals to our congregations. With reference to the considerate kindness of Miss Hollond for those whom no one else would have thought of, as needing aid, or being within reach of it, there can be no question. And if what she did in this regard ever came abroad, it was not of her connivance.

For a year or two she had been losing ground and while spending the summer of 1870 at Cresson Springs, was taken sick, with what seemed to be a severe attack of indigestion, but which proved to be a new development of her subtle heart disease. For a day or two she seemed to improve, but on the 9th of August, 1870, she suddenly grew worse, and in the early morning fell asleep. Three days after, her remains were borne to the cemetery at Laurel Hill, followed by a large concourse of true mourners. The funeral services were conducted by Drs. W. M. Rice and Samuel T. Lowrie.

Miss Elizabeth Potts, who has been connected with the school for a number of years as one of its most valued teachers, CHARLES E. MORRIS has kindly prepared the following sketch which will be read with appreciation not only by those who knew and loved Mr. Morris, but by all who have an interest in Hollond :

Among the men who have done so much for Hollond Sunday-school in the past there has been perhaps no more vivid personality than that of Mr. Charles E. Morris, who for eight years was its beloved superintendent and who left behind him influences for good which have never faded away. An earnest, consecrated Christian, he was inspiring in his very presence. Always cheery and bright, and full of enthusiasm, he exercised a stimulating influence upon all who came in contact with him. His deep spirituality and earnestness were combined with a shrewd common sense and a great degree of tact which eminently fitted him to be a leader.

When he was elected superintendent, he took

CHARLES ELLIS MORRIS

days for consideration and prayer, and during
that time his mother said that he could neither
eat nor sleep. With his coming, the school,
which knew only the old-time ways, took a
long step forward.

Himself an old-fashioned Presbyterian in
thought and doctrine, a worthy product of
careful home training, and of the instructions
of his revered and oft-quoted preceptor, Dr.
Mark Hopkins, president of Williams College,
at which institution he passed his student life,
he was the first superintendent to introduce
modern features into the school.

The use of an order of service, responsive
readings, silent prayer, the young people's society and the parents' and children's meetings
were all started by him. Trained by Dr.
Hopkins' lectures on the subject, he was enthusiastic in regard to the value of the Shorter
Catechism and made its study prominent in the
school.

When asked to become superintendent, he
made it one of his conditions that the teachers
should give up any engagement requiring them
to hasten away, and be willing to devote the
afternoon to the school and its interests, looking up absentees, visiting the sick, etc.

By his great earnestness and his strong personal magnetism, he was able to carry his
teachers with him. He trained them to feel

that they should be a unit in purpose; that each teacher was responsible not only for his class, but for the general welfare of the school. He impressed upon us that the salvation of the souls of our pupils was the ultimate aim, without which our teaching was of small account. In his own addresses from the desk he made most vivid the claims of the gospel, and left the impression that personal salvation alone was vitally important.

Mr. Morris thought a Sunday-school without a teachers' meeting was an anomaly, and he brought about the establishment of weekly meetings for the study of the lesson, and so impressed us with the necessity that the attendance was large. Teachers who habitually absented themselves were thought very neglectful of duty. We prepared our own lesson papers for the use of the school, for a time, in those days before the establishment of the International lessons. We often held the meetings at the homes of some of the teachers, and full parlors indicated the general interest. The lessons were made so delightful and instructive that the evening was to many of us the pleasantest of the week.

Mr. Morris would often come to the business meetings full of some new plan or suggestion which he would lay before the teachers. Opportunity was always given for the fullest and freest discussion, which sometimes became quite heated. Strong opposition would often melt away before his explanations. No plan, however, was put into operation except with the consent and vote of the majority.

Mr. Morris came among us as a young man, in fullest sympathy with the young, and so entered into the life and interests of every pupil. He had a hearty, cheery way of greeting all, which roused the utmost enthusiasm for him on the part of the pupils. On occasions of entertainment, he was full of life and fun, ready to lead in games and to rouse abundance of merriment; but when he took his place on the platform, his very presence controlled the school, and there was but small effort required to keep order. The pupils, one and all, loved him. One of the older pupils said recently, ''I reverenced Mr. Morris.'' Every pupil was sure of his friendly sympathy, and with the comparatively small numbers, he could know nearly all individually. A young girl about to join the church said: ''I never thought much of my need of a Saviour until Mr. Morris said, ' Annie, I wish you were a Christian,' and then I felt that if Mr. Morris cared about it, it was quite time for me to think about it myself.'' It was at Mr. Morris's suggestion that regular competitive examinations upon the lessons were held for a time, and some pupils passed with a very high grade.

In his public addresses Mr. Morris was strong and vigorous. He always held the attention of his audience without apparent effort. In his summing up of the lesson, he would seize upon one or two of the leading points and make an intensely practical appeal, which left its impress upon the memory. It was because of Mr. Morris's urgent desire, that we decided to celebrate Christmas by giving, rather than by receiving gifts, although he himself did not live to see the experiment tried.

It was largely owing to Mr. Morris's efforts and faith that the Hollond chapel was built. The neighborhood of Tenth and Carpenter streets had so largely become settled by Roman Catholics that no further growth was possible. When Miss Hollond died in 1870 she left us $10,000, conditional upon our building in a more promising location within five years. Two years had elapsed, with no steps taken, when Mr. Morris, by his statements to Dr. Boardman and the session of the Tenth Church, induced them to endorse an appeal to the members of the congregation for additional funds. This, with the personal efforts of Mr. Morris and some of the teachers among outside friends, resulted in securing a sum sufficient to supplement Miss Hollond's legacy and purchase a lot and build the chapel. He took great delight in planning the house and greatly rejoiced when we entered into possession.

His faith in the future of the church to be was very strong, and he often spoke confidently of the day when a South Broad Street Presbyterian Church would stand upon the corner. Although the name was claimed by another church before we were ready to build, he would rejoice as fully in seeing there the Harriet Hollond Memorial Church.

Mr. Morris's activity was so great, and he accomplished so much, it is hard to realize that he was only thirty-five years of age at the time of his death. His funeral services were held in the Tenth Church, on Thursday, 13th February, 1879, at which the school attended, a choir of the older scholars leading the singing. The addresses on that occasion by Hollond Sunday-school workers, as well as the touching resolutions adopted by the teachers and officers of Hollond school, are included in the memorial volume published soon after his death. He is further commemorated in the fine stained-glass window at the east end of the church, and also by a bronze tablet above the superintendent's desk in the chapel, which bears the following inscription :

IN MEMORIAM

OUR SUPERINTENDENT

CHARLES E. MORRIS

Born March 7th, 1844
Died Feb. 10th, 1879

Be thou faithful unto death and
I will give thee a crown of life.

———

On the 17th of May, 1877, Mr. Morris married Miss Ella Graham Benson. One child, a daughter, was born to them. Mrs. Morris has long been a faithful teacher in the school. She has frequently manifested her interest in the church by liberal contributions. Recently the daughter, Miss Margaretta, became a member of our teaching force and has entered upon the work with characteristic devotion.

"Among those still active who have been the longest time identified with the Hollond work and the most useful in it," Dr. J. R. Miller writes, " no one has wrought more faithfully or more efficiently, and no one has endeared himself to more hearts, than Mr. William L. DuBois. As an officer of the Tenth Presbyterian Church, he was deeply interested in the promotion of the work at Hollond while it was still a mission. No one did more than he to keep the heart of the mother-church warm toward the child and to secure year by year

WILLIAM L. DUBOIS

the generous support necessary for the maintenance of the Sunday-school ; for whi e the church services in those earlier days were supported by the Hollond people themselves, the expenses of the school were borne by the Tenth Church—an annual collection and subscription being taken for this purpose.

" In the final disposition of the proceeds of the sale of the old Tenth Church, when it had decided to unite with the West Spruce Street Church, Mr. DuBois was one of the friends in that church who represented and advocated the Hollond interests and to whom Hollond is indebted for the large share which came to it to aid in the completion of the new building and to provide the handsome endowment fund which will aid so much in the work of the future. Hollond cannot be too grateful to Mr. DuBois for his personal influence and wise help in these and other ways. He did much, far more than many persons know, to give it its favorable beginning and its fine equipment as a church.

" For many years, the work of Mr. DuBois in the Sunday-school has been invaluable. Though never connected with the church as an organization—his membership and official relation having always been and still continuing with the Tenth Church—he has always wrought and still works in the school. He has long served and still serves as the Sunday-school treasurer, giving careful thought to financial matters. As counsellor in all the business affairs of the school, he has ever been wise and faithful. As a teacher, his services have been of great value and have been fittingly appreciated. He has won a place in the hearts of the many who have been in the classes taught by him; and he will long be cherished by them as a personal friend—sympathetic, kindly, thoughtful, and ready to help in any possible way.

"Mr. DuBois is a quiet man. His voice is not often heard in public meetings; but his work is of the kind that builds up and endures, and his influence is always for good."

At a conference of Hollond workers held in the chapel in the fall of 1897, Mr. DuBois spoke on "The Pioneers of Hollond." He said in part :

"This work, once known as the Moyamensing Mission, which began in such a small way—first in the little building on Christian street and afterwards in the Carpenter street building—has shown itself to be under God's especial care. When we contemplate the smallness of that beginning and the great church into which it has developed, with all its accessories which are represented here to-night, truly we are filled with the deepest gratitude

to God for all that he has done for us.   My
own connection with the Mission began in the
year 1866.   I believe that the only teachers
and officers now in the work who were teachers
then, beside myself, are Miss Penrose, Mr. and
Miss Cooke, and Miss Rivell.   The work was
full of discouragement, but the old Tenth
Church came to our help nobly—supplying us
with needed funds, and giving us teachers.
Especially were we assisted and encouraged by
Miss Hollond's support.''

Mr. DuBois closed by paying a high tribute
to the worth of Mr. Charles E. Morris.   He
explained that it was altogether due to the
energy of Mr. Morris that the conditions of
Miss Hollond's will were met and the money
applied to the erection of our chapel building.

The following sketch of the Rev. Louis
Rodman Fox, who was directly connected with
the Hollond field from 1872 to
REV. LOUIS 1874, was prepared by a close
R. FOX personal friend : Mr. Fox was
born at Doylestown, Pa., January
10, 1834, and was educated in Philadelphia at
the school of the Rev. Samuel Wylie Crawford,
D. D.   Later, Mr. Fox attended Brown University, after which he studied and entered
upon the practise of law, but his heart turned
continually to the ministry and he prepared

himself for it at Princeton Theological Seminary in the class of 1859.

He began his ministry at a little mission station at Bustleton, near Burlington, N. J., where he afterwards spent five additional years, leaving the church in possession of a beautiful building, erected through his instrumentality, free of debt. He spent a year in laborious mission work at Tuckerton and Bass River, N. J., and was for a time on a special service of the Christian Commission in our Civil War. His regular pastorates were in Washington, D. C., Philadelphia and Detroit. That in Philadelphia began in January, 1872, when he was called from the North Church of Washington to be associate pastor with the Rev. Henry A. Boardman, D.D., in the pastorate of the Tenth Church. Here he labored with great diligence, preaching with acceptance and profit, and doing most faithful pastoral work.

Mr. Fox was especially active and helpful in connection with the Moyamensing Mission of the church, and his first preaching service there, which antedated by several days his installation by Presbytery at the Tenth Church, was the first preaching service held after the re-organization of the Sunday-school. His interest in the enterprise never flagged. He held frequent services both on Sundays

REV. LOUIS R. FOX

and during the week, and soon found that
meetings for inquirers were necessary. In
the following March, Mr. Charles E. Morris
wrote to a friend: ''Scholars from our school
are coming into the church. We ought to be
much encouraged.'' As there was no church
organization, these were enrolled as members
of the parent church until March 24, 1882,
when the Hollond Church was organized.
When other duties would permit of it, Mr.
Fox was often found teaching a class in the
Sunday-school. He was instrumental in raising much of the money to supplement Miss
Hollond's bequest, thus securing the erection
of the new chapel on Federal street.

In 1874, Mr. Fox resigned his connection
with the Tenth Church but always took a
deep interest in the work of the mission. It
was a pleasure to him that he was able to
take part in the dedication of the Hollond
Memorial Chapel, February 15, 1874, when he
preached the evening sermon from the text,
''*Whosoever will, let him take the water of
life freely;*'' and also in that of the Hollond
Church on October 15, 1893, when he made
an address full of reminiscences of the past
and of gratitude to God for the prosperity of
the present, to the throng which filled the
large and handsome building.

Mr. Fox's last pastorate was in Detroit,

Michigan, where, with that missionary spirit so characteristic of his whole ministerial life, he devoted himself to the organization and up-building of a work which had been chaotic and unpromising. This church is now known as the Church of the Covenant, and has a beautiful house of worship, the result of his efforts. "He consecrated unusual gifts and acquirements to the preaching of the gospel to the poor. He identified himself with rare tact and Christian sympathy with the interests and sufferings of his people. He was among them always and gave himself for them. And he had his reward in that out of that faithful work there are many shining jewels that one day will be resplendent in his crown. He was a devoted friend, staunch and true, whose ready wit and quaint humor, well stored mind and kindly heart found everywhere a cheery welcome. He was a Christian who realized Christ daily, and so believed His promise and so loved Him that the passion of his life was to preach to others that promise of love."

In 1890, protracted ill health compelled him to lay down his work and retire to his Philadelphia home, from whence, on December 21, 1894, he was called, not to fresh and coveted labors but to the immediate presence of the Master to receive his reward.

Dr. J. R. Miller pays this tribute to his memory:

" Mr. Fox was a man of lovable spirit. His friendships were deep, strong and lasting. He was much interested in young men, especially in those who were preparing for the ministry. He was wise and faithful as a pastor, and his touch is on many lives.

"All who are interested in Hollond have special reason to remember Mr. Fox with love and gratitude. The period of his co-pastorate in the Tenth Church included the time when the money was being raised to supplement Miss Hollond's bequest for the building of our Sunday-school chapel. Mr. Fox took a very deep interest in this work, and, in company with Mr. Charles E. Morris, visited the people of the Tenth Church to solicit subscriptions. His heart was in the mission, for which he often preached, besides rendering aid in many other ways. We will long cherish his memory. There are those among us who have been helped and blessed by his life in the past, who will carry in our hearts the influence of his friendship and of his words for many days."

It is pleasant to record that the hearty encouragement which Mr. Fox gave to the work is being perpetuated by the faithful teaching of Mrs. Fox in the Sunday-school—a loving service which is fully appreciated.

In the death of Samuel M. Kennedy, one of
our elders, which occurred early on Tuesday
morning, July 25th, 1893, our
SAMUEL M.   church lost a valued and useful
KENNEDY   member. The session took the
following action :

"Mr. Kennedy was one of the four elders
chosen at the time of the organization of the
church, in March, 1882.   During all the years
of his service he was faithful, not only in his
attendance upon the regular meetings of the
session, but in all the duties of his office.   In
his personal life he was singularly blameless
and true; a man of gentle heart, of loving spirit;
thoughtful, unselfish, kind, yet of strong con-
victions and unflinching steadfastness.   As a
church member he was exemplary ; always in
his place, a devout worshiper, and prepared for
every good work.   As a church officer, he was
faithful in all duties, wise in counsel, discreet,
spiritually-minded, cordial in all his relations,
having favor with the people.   His death has
disclosed, in a way not even suspected before, his
wide personal influence in the community. Hundreds of lives will carry forever the impress of
his life and the memory of his words and acts."

On the following Sunday evening, July 30th,
Dr. Miller preached a memorial sermon from
the text : "He was a good man." Acts 11: 24.
A few extracts are here given :

SAMUEL M. KENNEDY

"Mr. Kennedy was a friend of those who were trying to recover themselves from a sinful past. We all know his deep interest in the temperance cause. Never did any young man, trying to free himself from the bondage of the drink habit, turn in vain to him for sympathy, brotherly love, and help.

" He was a man without envy. It gave him no pain to see others of his fellow-workers promoted and publicly honored even above himself. Indeed, he seemed to rejoice more in the honor that came to others than that which gathered about himself. He wrought solely for Christ. Every other name shone in pale light before his eyes in comparison with the splendors that burned about the name of Christ. He shrank from positions which would seem to give him prominence. Well do I remember when I spoke first to him about becoming an elder. Our church was about to be organized, and he was one of the four men of whom all the people thought for elders. I told him of this desire, and it seemed almost to give him pain. He said he had not the needed qualifications, and begged me not to permit his name to be used. I spoke to him more fully of it saying that it was evidently the call of God to him. When the time came, and he was unanimously chosen, he quietly came forward to be set apart for the sacred office ; and we all know with what a loving and beautiful spirit he discharged the duties of this position until he was called up higher.

"On the floral tribute sent by the Young People's Society of Christian Endeavor were these words: 'Faithful Always.' These words carry the secret of his life. He was always faithful to God. He never forgot a promise, nor failed to keep an engagement. He did his work conscientiously—the smallest things as carefully as the greatest. Far more than any of us know does such minute and painstaking faithfulness build up beautiful character, and make a life bright and holy."

Few men have met with greater success in their life's work than Dr. Miller. He was born on a farm in Beaver county, Pa., of Scotch-Irish ancestry. As a rule it is a good thing to be born a farmer's boy and to come of Scotch-Irish stock. Dr. Miller's career gives emphasis to the rule. He has won well-deserved distinction as a pastor, a teacher and an author. His name is a household word in thousands of homes, and his uplifting spiritual teachings have endeared him to thousands of hearts. He was graduated in 1862 from Westminster College, New Wilmington, Pa., and then spent two years and a half in the work of the Christian Commission, being connected

DR. J. R.
MILLER

chiefly with the Army of the Potomac. In 1867 he graduated from the United Presbyterian Theological Seminary, Allegheny, Pa.

Dr. Miller's first charge was at New Wilmington, where he remained for two years. He then accepted a call to the Bethany Presbyterian Church, Philadelphia, where he remained for nine years. It was during his early ministry in Bethany (1870) that he married Miss Louise E. King, of Argyle, New York. Three children have been born to them. In 1878 he was installed pastor of the Broadway Presbyterian Church, Rock Island, Illinois. He relinquished this charge in 1880 to connect himself with the editorial work of the Presbyterian Board of Publication, Philadelphia. During the same year his Alma Mater conferred upon him the degree of Doctor of Divinity.

January 2nd, 1881, Dr. Miller began his work in the Hollond field. On the 24th of March, 1882, the Mission was organized into the Hollond Memorial Church, and Dr. Miller was installed as its first pastor April 23rd, of the same year. The pastoral relation was dissolved September 3rd, 1883, in order that he might devote himself more fully to his duties in connection with the Board of Publication.

Dr. Paden succeeded Dr. Miller, and was installed pastor November 20th, 1883. He labored alone for awhile but the work continued to increase so rapidly that Dr. Miller, at the request of the session and the trustees, returned in January, 1886, to assist in the field, still keeping up his connection with the Board.

During Dr. Paden's enforced absence in 1892, recuperating his health, the pastoral work was carried on by Dr. Miller. As a token of their appreciation, the congregation presented him with a handsome oak library suit, consisting of a desk, couch, book-case, rocker and chairs.

On the 27th of March, 1893, Dr. Miller left Philadelphia on his first vacation in thirteen years. He travelled with the Hon. John Wanamaker through the Pacific states. He had a pleasant experience in San Francisco: Going into the home of a Christian Chinese, the man said, "I know you well, for I have read your books," and from a near-by table he brought to the Doctor several of his works. On his return, the Pastors' Aid Society gave him a reception in the chapel on the 18th of May.

The first sermon in the new church was preached by Dr. Miller on Monday evening, October 16th, 1893, from the text, "*Jesus Christ, the same yesterday, and to-day, and forever.*"

On the 1st of July, 1896, Dr. Miller sailed

with his family from New York on the St. Paul for a two months' vacation tour of Europe, going as far south as Naples. The Christian Endeavor Society gave him a parting reception. The chapel was crowded and many of the church organizations presented him with flowers, accompanied with appropriate sentiments. He returned to Philadelphia on the 26th of August, and was given a hearty reception by the congregation on the 28th.

On the fourteenth of October, 1897, Dr. Miller wrote to the session resigning the work which they had invited him to take up years before. He was, however, at the request of the session, appointed moderator by the Presbytery, until a pastor could be secured to take the place made vacant by his and Dr. Paden's resignations. He continued with us until after the call to Dr. Martin had been accepted. His last sermon was delivered on Sunday evening, June 5th, 1898.

He ended his connection with us by conducting the Christian Endeavor consecration service on the following Tuesday evening. A number of earnest, heart-felt talks were made in which the speakers gave expression to the affection they had for him and told of some of the many ways in which he had helped them. It was specially fitting that he should receive these loving tributes in the room which had witnessed so many of his most active efforts to inspire in others truer ideals of living.

It was no small thing for such a man to give seventeen years of his life to the service of one church; and such a service as but few churches are ever blessed with.   He was to all of us the faithful pastor, the wise leader, the generous helper, the safe counselor, and the resourceful friend.   No one deserving of help and sympathy ever appealed to him in vain.   Whittier's lines apply to him with singular fitness :

" With us was one who, calm and true,
    Life's highest purpose understood ;
And, like his blessed Master, knew
    The joy of doing good."

Mr. Henry A. Walker thus writes of Dr. Miller's connection with Hollond : " His pulpit work commanded our respect and admiration.   In these days when sensationalism holds such a prominent place in so many of our churches, we need to be thankful that there are men who do no ' show preaching.' Rugged earnestness, backed by sincere living, is the only preaching that counts.

"In the practical dealings of life, when the hard pushed needed sympathy and encouragement, his work was strong in splendid results; and when the final roll is called, it will be found that this type of man has lived the biggest and best because he has grasped the Christ idea of service.

" Dr. Miller's work in our church was most timely. In the critical periods, when a strong, capable man was needed at the helm; he was equal to all emergencies. He has always had enlarged conceptions of what the whole Hollond work should be. For his work, and for all that he has been to us, we are grateful."

Dr. Miller fills his position as editorial superintendent of the Board of Publication and Sunday-school Work with marked ability and to the entire satisfaction of the Church. The Westminster Teacher, of which nearly one hundred thousand copies are issued each month, receives a large share of his personal attention, and is a treasured help to Sunday-school teachers all over the land. He has written between twenty-five and thirty books, and he is to-day one of the best known and most widely read religious writers of America. His name is also a familiar one in Great Britain, where more than a quarter of a million copies of his works have been sold. These works have been translated into German, French, Japanese and Hungarian.

Dr. Miller is a forceful and popular writer. His thoughts leave a lasting impress upon the hearts and minds of his readers because he writes of life as he finds it—in the homes of happiness and affluence, and in the homes of the lowly, the discouraged, and the tempted.

Here he gives a glimpse of joy, there a bit of heart-break, but never for an instant does he lose sight of the all-absorbing purpose of his writing—to encourage the hopeless, to uplift the fallen, and to inspire in all a holy desire for truer and nobler living. In all his writings there is fullness of strength and helpfulness, and those who follow his teachings cannot fail to have

" Promptings their former life above,
And something of a finer reverence
For beauty, truth, and love.''

It is doubtless true that " there is no royal road to learning,'' but it is none the less true that one may win his way to learning right royally, and this is what Dr. Paden did.

DR. WILLIAM M. PADEN

He was born in Washington county, Pa. His father was of Scotch and his mother of Pennsylvania Dutch extraction. He worked on the farm during the summer months and early acquired a passion for nature. For a few midwinters he went to the district school and then rode nearly five miles to recite Latin and algebra to his pastor, Dr. J. S. Marquis. He attended a summer session of the Canons- burg Academy, and then taught the home school for three winters, continuing his sum- mer studies at the academy, diligently prepar- ing for college. By 1875 he was ready to enter the sophomore class, but at this time a professorship was offered to him in the Canonsburg Academy, which he accepted and taught Latin and Greek there for three years. He entered the junior class of Princeton University, without conditions, in 1878, and graduated with honors two years later.

During his college course, he took the first Junior Orator Medal and the $120.00 prize for best written oration ; was editor of the Nassau Literary Magazine in his senior year ; took two medals for essays, and won a $100.00 Lynde Debate Prize. He was the superintendent of the Stony Brook Sunday-school during his college course, and of the First Church Sunday-school, Princeton, during his seminary course. He had three calls, besides the one from Hollond, during his senior year, and received eight calls during his Hollond pastorate.

Dr. Paden graduated from Princeton Seminary in the spring of '83, and spent the summer travelling in Europe. He entered upon the Hollond work on the first Sunday of October of that year, and was installed on the twentieth of the following November. In 1888, he was a delegate to the World's Conference of the Young Men's Christian Associations, held at Stockholm, Sweden. He spent the first nine months of 1892 in the South recuperating his health. He had the degree of Doctor of Divinity conferred upon him in 1895. He sailed for Paris November 21st, 1895, on a six months' leave of absence, to take charge of a movement having for its main object the reaching of the English-speaking students in the Latin Quarter of that city. He returned June 5, 1896, and on the following Monday evening a pleasant reception was tendered him under the auspices of the Pastor's Aid Society and the Ushers' Association.

He spent his summer vacation of 1897 in Salt Lake City, Utah, and preached in the First Presbyterian Church there. After his return to Philadelphia he received, and finally determined to accept, a call from that congregation. This decision he announced from the pulpit on Sunday morning, October 3d, when he said, in part :

" You have heard, I am sure, of a call I have had to Salt Lake City. It has come to me in such a way that I am bound to consider it.

" I do not expect to find a larger place in any other people's affections ; you have given me a support and sympathy which I can hardly expect to find where my lot may be cast during the coming years. Nor do I think of leaving you because another church has taken a larger place in my affections ; I go among strangers, or among acquaintances of a few weeks' standing. My tried affections are all here. This has

been the church of my first love, and into it I
have built some of the best years of my life. I
know every stone in this building. I have
stood on these walls from the foundation to the
roof. * * * The membership of the Salt Lake
church is scarcely larger than the membership
of Hollond when I came here, and the church
accommodations are inferior to our accommodations fourteen years ago. The necessities of
the field are, however, most urgent, and its
place in the metropolis of the great intermoun-
tain region and in the capital of one of our
youngest and most interesting states is unique-
ly important. The church has also a most important place as situated at the headquarters
of Mormonism, and at the very head of the
Gentile work among this peculiar people. The
call has come to me with prayerful emphasis
and phenomenal unanimousness ; all this, with
the unique importance of the field to our Christian work has had much to do with its favorable consideration. * * * I believe that I am
under God's orders to go, and the announcement of this morning is made that you may
join with me in asking Presbytery that I be
released to obey orders.''

In view of this statement, and not in accordance with their feelings, the congregation
yielded to the request, and on Sunday evening,
October 17th, Dr. Paden preached his final

sermon as our pastor. On the following Wednesday evening a farewell reception was given him by the Ushers' Association, which was very largely attended.

The following editorial appeared in the *Presbyterian Journal* of October 21st :

" While the brethren and friends of the Rev. Dr. Paden in Philadelphia sincerely regret his departure from their immediate circle and companionship, and mourn with the Hollond Church the sundering of near and dear and valued relations, at the same time they are gratified that he goes to occupy a position so important and so far-reaching in its influence to Church and State, as the pastorate to which he is invited in Salt Lake City. Many prayers will follow him, and we can assure him that the Presbyterian Church of Philadelphia and vicinity will watch with great interest his work as pastor and citizen of Utah."

Mr. Robert H. Preston thus writes of Dr. Paden in his relation to the young men of Hollond :

" He has profoundly and permanently affected our intellectual life. His mind has put many of us in living and loving touch with a large and beautiful world of thought ; his spirit has quickened in us a noble discontent with unrefined and unrefining relations ; his view of the possibilities of young men—especially those employed during the day—have fired many of us with new longings after a higher intellectual standard. In a word, he has revealed our deeper self to ourselves, and the revelation has become the power which has sent us onward and upward towards a nobler ideal of life.''

Dr. Paden gave the very heart of his life to Hollond, and no one could question his devotion to its interests. He early won and easily held the affections of his people. To the work of erecting the new church he gave himself and his means unreservedly. He was specially anxious that the building should stand on the site it now occupies, and to the attainment of that desire he used his utmost endeavor.

He was never lacking in those finer qualities which kindle in other men aspirations for better living. If he loved to develop the intellectual it was that the spiritual also might '' grow from more to more.'' Of him it could be said—

> '' he spake of men
> As one who found pure gold in each of them.
> He spake of women just as if he dreamed
> About his mother ; and he spoke of God
> As if he walked with Him and knew His heart.''

Higher praise than this cannot be given—he honored mankind, reverenced womanhood, and walked with God.

In our Christian Endeavor meetings he was

specially earnest and tender. He was rarely absent. Our cozy "upper room" had for him an inexpressible charm. Surrounded as he was by the love of his young people, he frequently gave the fullest expression to his feelings, revealing a heart rich in spiritual experience, and a whole-souled charity which brought us all into closer and more reverent touch with the Eternal. His rare spiritual gifts and his splendid intellectual attainments combine to make of him a man to be honored as a pastor, to be proud of as a friend—a man to be forever held in grateful remembrance by all who have known and loved him, and who have felt his helpful touch upon their lives.

———

Dr. Paden has been very successful in Utah. During his first year above one hundred members united with his church, and an old debt of $10,000 was canceled. He is to-day one of the ablest anti-Mormon leaders of the country.

Our present pastor, Dr. George Edward Martin, preached for us for the first time on the 24th of April, 1898, and at **DR. GEORGE EDWARD MARTIN** a congregational meeting held in the chapel on the 10th of the following month, he received a unanimous call to our pulpit.

Dr. Martin was born in Norwich, Connecticut. He was graduated from Yale in 1872.

REV. GEORGE E. MARTIN, D. D.

After a theological course at the Yale Seminary, he was installed pastor over the Centre Congregational Church of Brattleboro, Vermont, July 9th, 1879. After a successful pastorate of four years in this church he was called to the First Congregational Church of Brockton, Massachusetts, and was installed October 11th, 1883. He remained in charge of this church less than a year, leaving it to accept the pastorate of the First Presbyterian Church, St. Louis, Missouri, over which he was installed in October, 1884. Here he labored for fourteen years and made a splendid record. He was moderator both of the Synod of Missouri and of the Presbytery of St. Louis. He was greatly interested in educational matters and was officially connected with several institutions of learning. He accepted the call to our church, and was installed pastor October 17, 1898. Dr. S. W. Dana, pastor of the Walnut Street Church and moderator of the Presbytery of Philadelphia, presided, and proposed the constitutional questions. Rev. E. P. Terhune, D.D., preached the sermon; Dr. Samuel A. Mutchmore (who died thirteen days later) delivered the charge to the people, and Dr. Charles A. Dickey made the charge to the pastor. Dr. J. R. Miller delivered the installation prayer.

On the following Wednesday evening the

Ushers' Association gave Dr. and Mrs. Martin a pleasant reception. Many floral tributes were presented by the several church organizations.

Dr. Martin made an earnest address in which he expressed the hope that the bond of union between himself and his people might grow stronger and more helpful, and that great good might be accomplished by both pastor and people in their united efforts to do the Master's will.

On the 1st of June, 1882, Dr. Martin was married to Miss Emily Herrick, who was born in Tirumangalam, South India, where her father was a missionary. She has charge of our largest adult Sunday-school class. In many other ways also she is giving important service to the work.

Dr. Martin received the degree of D. D. from two colleges—Wabash and Park. He is a talented musician, and is specially interested in preparing music for children. He is also the author of several books, among them being an attractive little volume, entitled ''Sermons and Sermon Rhymes.'' In '' Sunday Songs for Little Children,'' recently issued by the Presbyterian Board of Publication and Sabbath-school Work, Dr. Martin displays his remarkable versatility by successfully entering three great fields of culture—poetry, music, and decorative art. The pages are adorned with dainty marginal designs, and each song is accompanied with an appropriate illustration which puts into visual form the spirit of the words. The art work is Dr. Martin's, and with but few exceptions, the words and music also are his.

Dr. Martin is an able preacher. His fine command of language enables him to express his thoughts in choicest speech. His broad culture, ripe scholarship, refined manner, and long experience should make him a leader of whom any church might be proud. As the pastor of the First Church, St. Louis, he was unusually successful. He found it in uncongenial quarters with less than 250 members and with scarcely any organized activities ; he left it in new and commodious buildings, with nearly 700 members, and with a number of organizations thoroughly equipped for aggressive work. This gratifying change was due almost entirely to Dr. Martin's efforts.

With God's favor, and with the hearty cooperation of our congregation, Dr. Martin should easily repeat his fine record. It is pleasant to know that he is growing in favor with his people—especially with those who are "shut in" and who are thus in a position fully to appreciate his kindly ministry.

We will serve God best, and best advance the highest interests of our beloved church, by

being true to the leadings of the Holy Spirit,
and by uniting heartily and prayerfully in all
plans that have for their aim the upbuilding of
a broader, deeper, truer spiritual life in this
portion of our city.   We believe in the ability
of Dr. Martin, and we have confidence in the
loyalty of our people. We doubt not that God
has a great work for us to do.   We are all
'' workers together '' with Him.   We face the
future gratefully, hopefully, courageously.
'' Let us play the men for our people, and
for the cities of our God; and the Lord do
that which seemeth him good.''

The Rev. Leslie L. Overman occupied the
pulpit as Dr. Martin's assistant for the first
time on the 5th of December,
REV. L. L.   1898, and took an active part in
OVERMAN   the service.

Mr. Overman is a native of
Ohio. He was graduated from the University
of Wooster, and took a post-graduate Philo-
sophical course at Princeton University.   His
theological training was received at the Princeton Theological Seminary, from which institution he was graduated in 1882.   He was
ordained by the Presbytery of Portsmouth,
Ohio, November 8th the same year.   He has
been pastor of the McNeily Presbyterian
Church, Nashville ; Montgomery Church,
Presbytery of Cincinnati ; Page Boulevard

REV. L. L. OVERMAN

Presbyterian Church, St. Louis; assistant pastor of the Lafayette Park Presbyterian Church, St. Louis, and assistant pastor of the Second Presbyterian Church, St. Louis.

Mr. Overman has had wide experience, and although he has been with us but a short time, has won our esteem by his genial manner and conscientious performance of duty. By his attention to the sick and by his visits to the homes of the congregation he is rendering valuable and effective service. During Dr. Martin's summer vacation, he had full charge of the field and zealously labored to meet the many demands made upon his time and strength.

It is earnestly hoped that under these our new leaders our beloved church will go forward to greater spiritual power and to larger usefulness.

Mr. Ogden's success in life and his all round usefulness afford excellent illustrations of the truthfulness of Shakespeare's assertion that

ROBERT CURTIS OGDEN

" Men at times are masters of their fates :
The fault, dear Brutus, is not in our stars,
But in ourselves, that we are underlings.''

His educational advantages were limited, as he left school and went to work before reaching the age of fourteen. He soon realized, how-

ever, the need of more thorough and practical
mental equipment, and determined to acquire
it by diligent study during the only time at his
command—after business hours. He was fortunate in securing the services of a wise and
sympathetic instructor, and by faithful application, when other boys were sleeping or play-
ing, he was enabled to secure a practical business education equal, if not superior in some
respects, to that possessed by many college
graduates. His association with intellectual
people was also of inestimable value to him.

In 1854, Mr. Ogden removed to New York.
He returned to Philadelphia in 1879 and soon
after became connected with the firm of John
Wanamaker.

During the civil war Mr. Ogden was a member of the 23rd New York Regiment. He
held commissions in that regiment, and also
on the staff of the Eleventh Brigade, of which
it was a part.

He is a member of a number of organizations,
among them being Meade Post No. 1, the
Union League, Manufacturers' Club, Presbyterian Social Union, Art Club and Contem-
porary Club, of this City; of the XX Century
and Hamilton Clubs, of Brooklyn; and of the
Pennsylvania Society, Union League, Century,
XIX Century, and National Arts Club, New
York City.

ROBERT C. OGDEN

For above a quarter of a century Mr. Ogden has had official connection with the Hampton Institute, Virginia, and for several years has been the president of its board of trustees. Much of its splendid usefulness has been due to his aggressive and enthusiastic efforts in its behalf. He is also a director of the Union Theological Seminary, New York.

In all the great movements in this city during the past decade which have had for their object the alleviation of human suffering, his has been the fine executive skill and the generous purse which have added much to their success—Johnstown (1889), Russia (1892), Philadelphia (1894), Armenia (1895-6), have each and all, in their time of need, been the recipients of his practical sympathy and aid.

He has rendered valuable service to the Church at large, notably through his membership in two of its Boards—Ministerial Relief and Publication and Sabbath-School Work. In 1885, he was a commissioner to the General Assembly.

Mr. Ogden is an earnest and forceful speaker, and his services in this direction are in frequent demand. On the 31st of May, 1892, he made the address at the unveiling of the monument at Johnstown to perpetuate the memory of the six hundred and thirty-seven unidentified dead who lost their lives in the great flood that swept through the Conemaugh Valley on the fateful 31st of May, 1889. During this address he said : " Glancing across the little slopes of these grassy graves, thinking of the history and the mystery, wondering why it was, and finding not in my mind nor in the teachings of other men any solution or explanation of the great tragedy, I can only in imagination sit with Mrs. Browning in a country church-yard, and, summing it all up, repeat her own sweet and comforting lines—

> " And I smiled to think God's greatness
> Flowed around our incompleteness,—
> Round our restlessness, His rest."

His closing thought was—

" Far better some deed of brotherhood to the living than rare flowers, costly monuments, and tender sentiments to the dead."

Mr. Ogden is also an able writer. Among his published works are, " Progressive Presbyterianism," " Pew Rents and the New Testament," " The Perspective of Sunday-school Teaching," " The Unveiling of the Monument to the Unknown Dead," and " Samuel Chapman Armstrong : A Memorial Address."

Mr. Ogden's letters to the *Hollond Reminder* from his summer home in Kennebunkport, Maine, were always deeply interesting, and had a virile force which enabled us to see almost with his own eyes his old favorite, the change-

less yet ever-changing ocean, of which he
never tired of writing, nor we of reading.
The following brief extract from one of these
letters is a fine example of his imaginative and
appreciative powers :

"In my wanderings here I often imagine
that Faber must have written his exquisite
Vox Angelica by the seaside.   Only in such
surroundings could he have called upon his
soul to hear the angelic songs swelling

'O'er earth's green fields and ocean's wave-beat
shore.'

"Only in the blackness of a night storm on
the water could he have felt the sadness that
breathes in the line :

'Darker than night life's shadows fall around us.'

"Only in a golden sunset by the sea could
he have thought :

'Far, far away, like bells at evening pealing,
    The voice of Jesus sounds o'er land and sea,
And laden souls, by thousands meekly stealing,
    Kind Shepherd, turn their weary steps to Thee.'

"And so on to the grand expectancy of
hopefulness with which the blessed hymn ends :

'Till morning's joy shall end the night of weeping,
And life's long shadows break in cloudless love.'

"Surely he got his heart lessons from the
gray days and the golden by the sea."

Mr. Ogden became our superintendent in
1879, and at the organization of the church in

1882, he was one of the four elected to the eldership. Some time later, when the board of trustees was formed, he also became a member of that body. He never permitted his intimate relation with the broader fields of action to serve as a pretext to neglect the no less important duties which came to him through these offices and to which his intimate knowledge of men and affairs and his wide business experience enabled him to bring executive ability of the highest order.

He was married on the 1st of March, 1860, to Miss Ellen Elizabeth Lewis. For a long while Mrs. Ogden was actively engaged in the work of the church, as a member of the choir; and of the school, as a teacher of the Primary Department. Their two daughters were also teachers in the school.

Although in close touch with many lines of our work, it may be safe to say that Mr. Ogden's most serious thought was given to the planning and erection of the new church building. To his matchless energy, cultivated taste, and whole-souled generosity, we are indebted for much of the completeness displayed in its construction. This love for church-building came to him naturally through a long line of ancestry. Away back in 1630, Richard Ogden, of good Puritan stock, came from England to this country and settled in Stamford, Connecticut. In an old colonial record, still extant, there is a contract made by Richard Ogden and his brother John, in 1642, to build a church in New Amsterdam, now New York. Mr. Ogden is a direct descendant from Richard Ogden, from whom he is six generations removed.

On the evening of the wedding of Mr. Ogden's parents, in August, 1833, an official member of the old Tenth Church called on his grandmother to get her signature to a letter addressed to Dr. Boardman, requesting him to become the pastor of that church. At that time, his grandmother (she being a widow) and her family of seven daughters and two sons, were all connected with the Tenth Church. Mr. Ogden has always taken special interest in the Boardman incident in view of the fact that he himself became an elder in the church which owes its being to the one over which Dr. Boardman was so long the pastor.

Of Mr. Ogden's love for Hollond it is almost needless to speak. In spite of his pressing business and social duties he was often at the mid-week prayer meetings ; and Sunday afternoons always found him, if in town, in command of the school. Of his liberality, our treasurer, Mr. Cooke, writes : '' I have often felt that it was hardly justice to Mr. Ogden to keep to myself the knowledge of his generosity to which our church and school owe so much.''

The annual receptions given by Mr. Ogden to the officers and teachers were always looked forward to with pleasure. We were not only received with genial hospitality but also had the additional pleasure of listening to helpful addresses from one or more distinguished speakers.

On the 4th of April, 1897, Mr. Ogden occupied the platform for the last time as superintendent. Having assumed charge of the Wanamaker store in New York, he found it impracticable to retain the leadership of the school. He continues, however, his official connection with the boards of the church.

The following appreciative sketch by Mr. H. A. Walker sets forth in much of its true light Mr. Ogden's former relation to the school :

I well remember the first day Mr. Ogden entered upon his duties as superintendent of Hollond school. When he arose to speak, after Mr. Cooke's introduction, he impressed me as stern, vigorous and forcible, and I wondered if he would win and hold the hearts of our scholars. In the eighteen years of his official connection with the school, how completely and fairly he won everybody is too well known to need any words of mine by way of emphasis. To analyze his work briefly is not easy, large as the subject is. Here are a few points that "he who runs may read:"

First. His tremendous honesty of purpose. He never believed eloquence any substitute for life and action. Behind the words was the man; no show or sham about any part of his work; no wooden fronts painted to imitate marble for him. Like a great rock, he stood for what is square and true. He helped in a very large degree to put the Hollond church and school upon a platform broad and fair—equal rights and privileges, without regard to social standing or financial means.

Second. He was able, to a wonderful degree. The school under his management reached its highest efficiency. His splendid personality, his brilliant mind, with its wealth of resources, the helpful, strong talks he gave from the desk Sunday after Sunday, were an inspiration to all. He told no silly, exaggerated, sentimental stories; he spoke the solid, manly truth. He hit hard and often, with no compromise with meanness or narrowness.

Third. His hopefulness and faith were contagious. He left no depressing influence. With him "To doubt would be disloyalty; to falter would be sin." He was the father of the "Free Church" idea—wide open doors; a gospel for all; give as God prospers. His broad conception of the work put it on a basis that has given it a commanding position in the Church throughout the country because of the rare financial methods that control it. He backed his faith with his dollars; not only then, but now. The average man called to another city would also feel called to drop his burden. In Mr. Ogden's case he continues his keen interest and gives substantial help.

Fourth. His contribution to the general life at Hollond was very wholesome; his influence uplifting. The dignity and kindliness of his life were inspiring. With his varied interests he could find time to carry a pitcher of soup a dozen squares to a sick boy—not once but a dozen times. Match it!

Fifth. He had a beginning, a middle, and an end to whatever he did. He felt the responsibility and importance of the office of superintendent; there was nothing slipshod about his work. He toiled for what he gave us. His vigor, enthusiasm and fidelity were refreshing.

Thank God for men of action; men of high purpose; men of fine influence; men who tie themselves to God's work because they love it; men of large outlook—with no limited horizon!

Mr. William L. Cooke became assistant superintendent of the school under Mr. Morris in 1871. He sustained this re- WILLIAM L. lation until November 1st, 1897, COOKE when he was elected, against his earnest protest, to the position of superintendent made vacant by the resignation of Mr. Ogden. He is one of the most active and conscientious men who have ever been connected with our work. His services as elder, trustee, treasurer, and superintendent, (all of which offices he now holds) have been invaluable. His interest in the school began with his earliest recollection and has grown stronger with each succeeding year. The church has no member more consistent, the school no worker more sincere. He is faithful to all life's duties, and is in every way worthy of the high esteem in which he is held.

At the organization of the South Branch Young Men's Christian Association, Mr. Cooke was elected to the presidency, and he has been elected continuously to that office since that time. Mr. Cooke is also a member of the Presbyterian Social Union, and a vice-president of the Sunday-school Superintendents' Association.

Although a busy man, Mr. Cooke makes it a rule to attend all the Sunday services, and also the Wednesday evening prayer-meetings.

He was one of the original members of the
Young People's Association, which for years
did much to advance the spiritual interests of
our young people, and which, a few years ago,
was merged into the Christian Endeavor Society, through which its uplifting influence
continues.

Mr. Cooke represents much that is best in
our church and school life. Few men have
labored more faithfully, and none more dis-
interestedly. His interest has never failed;
his faith has never faltered. He has no ambition greater than to see the Hollond work in
the forefront of spiritual usefulness.

With the exception of a change in the date,
an invitation somewhat similar to the following
has annually found its way to every officer and
teacher of Hollond:

" Mr. William L. Cooke requests the pleasure of your company at a social gathering of
the officers of the Hollond Memorial Church,
with the officers and teachers of the Sunday-
school, at his home, 1536 South Broad Street,
Philadelphia, Thursday evening, February 16,
1899."

This is Mr. Cooke's kindly method of keeping alive the memory of the occupancy of the
chapel by the school—February 15, 1874.
Aside from perpetuating the pleasant associations of the past, these annual gatherings
have a very practical value in increasing the

interest of officers and teachers in each other,
and in creating a bond of sympathy which
must necessarily have a wholesome and stimulating effect on the entire work.

Mr. Cooke is whole-souled and kindly. He
does his work with rare fidelity. In the sacred
circle of home he is the ideal brother; in the
business world he stands for whatever is manly,
straightforward, and honest; and in his religious life he is "an example of the believers—
in word, in conversation, in charity, in spirit,
in faith, and in purity."

Mr. Henry A. Walker has been connected
with the school from early childhood. He
was made associate superintendent
HENRY A. in October, 1886. He also holds
WALKER the office of elder and trustee. In
supplying classes with teachers, in helping to
maintain order, and in his general oversight,
his services have been of inestimable value to
the school ; while his practical business experience has made him a most useful member of
two of the church boards. He believes in the
gospel of hope, of cheer, of courage. He
has but little patience with the man who in-
sists on facing darkness rather than light.
He sets his ideals high, and, without ostentation, seeks to reach them. He has a strong
personality and his life has long since become
a compelling influence for good.

Mr. Walker is a member of the Presbyterian Social Union. In 1886, he was the first president of the Young People's Union of Philadelphia. He is an able and interesting speaker. That he is a forceful writer and that he is devotedly attached to the interests of the church are admirably shown in the following brief extracts from a paper read by him before the Ushers' Association May 25th, 1899 :—

" This church of ours—God bless it—is destined, I believe, to do a great work in this portion of the city. The work of the past, with its noble and inspiring influences, points to this result ; the present able and consecrated management points to it also. Sacrifice and service, past and present, yoked together must accomplish the purpose we hope for, long for, pray for—that this church may stand in this community with no uncertain message, with no unloving heart, with no compromise with evil.

" Let us be glad we have this opportunity for work. It is a rare one. Work in any well-organized church means splendid opportunities. Work develops ; work means character. I don't want to live a mean, narrow and shriveled life ; neither do you. I don't want anyone to discount my Christianity ; neither do you. It is a sorry thing for any man, and for the church to which he belongs, if his religion is so poor it does not help to make

himself, his church, and other men better.
Not what we have *gathered* but what we have
given counts in the ways of usefulness.

"We want men to believe in the future
of this church with all their hearts ; men who
will try to do something big and noble here ;
men who will feel that the success of this
whole work depends largely upon their own
personal relation to it.   Your work and my
work for this church ought to be better to-day
than yesterday ; better this week than last
week ; better this year than last year.   We
want to be concerned for its success ; we want
to be *hurt* by its failure.   'What does my
membership cost me in labor and self denial?'
That is the question each one of us should face.
We want enlarged work ; we want enlarged
thought.   We have got the plant, situated
just where it ought to be—where the current
of life is constant.   We have got the preacher.
You may come here four Sundays in a month
that has four, and five Sundays in a month
that has five, and hear sermons stimulating
and uplifting.   It is no sinecure to keep pace
with the needs of a congregation such as ours.
One man can't do it ; he should have the
hearty co-operation and the direct support of
every man, women and child connected with
this place.   Not for his own sake, but for the
Master's.

"I have no sympathy with the man who takes a pessimistic glance at this magnificent work. Such a look is cowardly ; such a look is disloyalty to God. So long as there is one empty seat in our church and our school, there is work for us ; so long as there is one life in this neighborhood unchurched, there is something for us to do. Help to lift a man and you lift yourself ; neglect a man and you hurt yourself. Nothing but our level best will suffice. The right spirit wont quail at the work of to-day. Assume some responsibility ; don't do anything unless you mean it ; don't say anything unless you feel it. Strength, sincerity, and individuality of character are worth striving for. We must think, must plan, must work and endure, to make our church the place it ought to be ! "

CHARTER

[The following is an exact copy of our Charter as amended in 1886. The original Charter was adopted in May, 1883.]

We whose names are hereunto subscribed having associated for the promotion of the cause of Religion by such means, especially the worship of Almighty God, as are usual and customary in congregations under the ecclesiastical jurisdiction of the General Assembly of the Presbyterian Church in the United States of America, and believing that it is essential to the permanent organization of such an association, that it should enjoy the powers, privileges and immunities of a Corporation or body politic in law, do hereby certify that we are all Citizens of the Commonwealth of Pennsylvania and have associated ourselves for the purpose of being formed into a Corporation of the First Class, under the provisions of the Act of Assembly of said Commonwealth entitled " An Act to provide for the incorporation and regulation of certain Corporations," approved the Twenty-ninth day of April A. D. 1874 and that the following shall be the objects, articles and conditions of the said Corporation :

Article First. The name, style and title of the said Corporation shall be " Harriet Hollond Memorial Presbyterian Church of the City of Philadelphia."

Article Second. The faith and government of the said Church, shall conform to the faith and government of the Presbyterian Church in the United States of America, and the real estate now owned, or which may be owned hereafter by this Corporation shall be forever held and used by a church and congregation which shall be connected with and under the care of the said Presbyterian Church in the United States of America.

Article Third. The place where the business of the said Corporation shall be transacted is in the City of Philadelphia and the said Corporation shall exist perpetually. There shall be no capital stock issued. The names and residents of the Subscribers are as follows, viz : Robert C. Ogden, 1708 Locust Street, Theodore H. Loder 1402 Wharton Street, James C. Taylor 1307 Federal Street, Hon. John K. Findlay 1152 South Broad Street and William L. Cooke 825 Ellsworth Street all of Philadelphia, Pennsylvania.

Article Fourth. The temporal affairs of this Church shall be managed by a Board of Nine

Trustees, and they shall meet within ten days after the annual election and shall choose from their own number a President, Secretary and Treasurer.

Article Fifth. An Election for Trustees shall be held upon the Third Monday of January Anno Domini One thousand eight hundred and eighty-five and upon the Third Monday of January, bi-ennially thereafter. At each election the Corporation shall elect three trustees to serve for the term of six years or until their successors are elected. For the purpose of organization Nine Trustees were elected on the Third Monday of January A. D. One thousand eight hundred and eighty-three, three of whom are to serve for two years from the date of their election, three for four years and the remaining three for six years, or in each case, until their successors are elected and the said Board was given power when organized to decide by lot the respective terms of its members. The Trustees so elected shall be the Trustees of the said Corporation for the said terms and the term of each member shall be as by the said lot determined. Any vacancies occurring in the Board of Trustees, by death resignation or otherwise, the Board shall have power to fill. If the said Corporation neglect or omit on the day of the bi-ennial election, to hold their election as aforesaid,

said Corporation shall not be dissolved by reason of such neglect or omission, but said election shall take place within one calendar month from said day; Provided that in all cases notice of the time and place of holding an election, stated or special, for Trustees, shall be given out in the Church on each of the two Sabbaths immediately preceding the day of the election, by the Minister officiating, or a person delegated for that purpose by the Board of Trustees. The names and residences of the present Trustees elected on the Third Monday of January A. D. One thousand eight hundred and eighty-three as aforesaid are as follows ; Robert C. Ogden 1708 Locust Street, Philadelphia, Pa., Theodore H. Loder 1402 Wharton Street Philadelphia, Pa., David Orr 1305 South Fifteenth Street Philadelphia, Pa., James C. Taylor 1307 Federal Street Philadelphia, Pa., Amos Dotterer 1325 South Broad Street Philadelphia Pa., Henry A. Walker, 1733 Reed Street Philadelphia, Pa., Hon. John K. Findlay 1152 South Broad Street Phila. Pa., William L. Cooke 825 Ellsworth Street Phila. Pa. and James M. Leo 1503 Dunganon Street Philadelphia Penna.

Article Sixth. Any male person of the age of twenty-one years, who is a citizen of this State and a lay member of this corporation and has contributed the sum of five dollars for the year immediately preceding the day of election, shall be eligible to the office of Trustee.

Article Seventh. All regular worshipers in this Church who have attained the age of eighteen years. and who shall have contributed, by pew rent or otherwise, at the rate of two dollars annually for at least six months ; and whose contributions shall be a matter of record ; and not in arrears, shall be members and qualified voters in this Corporation.

Article Eighth. The several officers of the Board of Trustees shall perform the duties usually pertaining to their respective offices. The Treasurer shall receive and account for all moneys belonging to said Corporation, and shall give ample security on his accepting the office, for the faithful discharge of his duties, he shall have his accounts settled annually, to be laid before the Corporation at the time of the annual meeting. and he shall pay no moneys, except in accordance with appropriations made by the Board, upon orders signed by the President and attested by the Secretary.

Article Ninth. The Board of Trustees shall hold stated meetings upon the Thursday after the third Monday of January and on the third Thurday of April, July and October, for the transaction of business. Special Meetings of the Board may be called at any time by the President, and it shall be his duty to call a special meeting upon the request in writing of at least three of the Trustees. Five Trustees shall form a quorum for the transaction of business, but a less number may adjourn from time to time.

Article Tenth. The board of Trustees, shall take charge of, and hold all the real and personal estate of this corporation—and shall receive rents, and dues of the Corporation, and the public Collections, keeping the house of Worship, and other property of the Church in repair—providing for the payment of the debts of the Church, and paying the salary of the Pastor, and employing and paying the salaries of the Chorister and Sexton—and paying current expenses necessary in maintaining public worship. The board of Trustees shall keep two correct and regular minutes of all their meetings, whether stated or special, and full true and correct accounts of all monies received and expended by them, which said minutes, and accounts, shall at all times be open to the inspection, of any three members of the Corporation, at the time entitled to vote for Trustees. They shall also produce a full statement of their accounts, receipts and vouchers, to be open to the inspection of all whom it may concern, on the day of the election of Trustees, one hour before the time specified for said election to commence.

Article Eleventh. The Board of Trustees shall have power to make all such ByLaws, Rules and Regulations from time to time as may be found necessary for their government and the support and management of the secular concerns and affairs of this Corporation. Provided that the said ByLaws, Rules and Regulations, or any of them, be not repugnant to the Constitution and Laws of the United States, to the Constitution and Laws of this Commonwealth, or to the Provisions of this Charter.

Article Twelfth. It shall be lawful for the Board of Trustees to agree upon and adopt a Seal with a suitable device for this Corporation, and the same to alter, break and renew at their pleasure.

Article Thirteenth. The Pastor of the Church shall be called according to the Constitution of the Presbyterian Church as aforesaid. He shall be elected by ballot and a majority of the whole number of votes cast shall be necessary to his election. Provided always, that notice of the time and place of holding such election whenever it shall be necessary, shall be given out in the Church on each of the two Sabbaths immediately preceding the day of election by the minister officiating, or a person delegated for that purpose by the Board of Trustees. All the qualified voters for

Trustees and all communicants in connection with the Church, who are in good and regular standing, shall be entitled to vote in the election of Pastor.

Article Fourteenth. The salary of the Pastor shall be fixed by a majority of the qualified voters for Pastor present at the meeting for his election, and immediately preceding thereto : and it shall not be altered unless by the consent of a majority of the qualified voters as aforesaid present at an annual or special meeting of the Congregation. Said salary shall be paid monthly in advance.

Article Fifteenth. The Elders and Deacons of the Church shall be elected by ballot, by the communicants in connection with the Church, who are in good and regular standing exclusively, and a majority of the whole number of votes cast shall be necessary to a choice.

Article Sixteenth. The Session of this Church shall have the superintendence and control of the singing, and should it be desirable at any time to engage professional services in connection with the Church music, the contract for the same may be made by the Board of Trustees but shall not be considered as valid without the duly recorded approval of the Session. They shall have control of all funds contributed for missionary and benevolent purposes and of all such spiritual matters

as appertain to the office of the eldership by
the form of government of the Presbyterian
Church in the United States of America. The
Deacons shall have charge and distribution of
any funds which may be collected or appro-
priated for the relief of the poor of the Church ;
and the Trustees shall pay over to them all
funds which may be collected or received by
the Trustees for such purposes.

Article Seventeenth. The Annual Meeting
of the Congregation shall be held on the third
Monday in January in each and every year,
when any matters of business shall be in order.
Special Meetings of the Congregation may be
held at any time upon the call of the Board of
Trustees, and it shall be the duty of the President upon the request in writing of three
members of the Corporation to call a special
meeting at any time. But, no business shall
be considered in order at any special meeting
unless such business has been distinctly specified in the notice hereinafter provided for.
No person other than the qualified voters for
Trustees shall be allowed to vote at any annual
or special meeting of the Congregation except
as herein otherwise expressly provided. Notice
of every annual or special meeting shall be
given out in the Church on each of the two
Sabbaths, immediately preceding such meeting,
by the Minister officiating or a person delegated

for that purpose by the Board of Trustees.

Article Eighteenth. The Board of Trustees shall keep a book in which shall be registered the subscriptions to the support of this Church of all the subscribing members of the Congregation and such record shall be the only evidence required as a qualification for voting as provided for in Article Seventh of this Charter. The book of the Session, certified by the Moderator or Clerk, shall be conclusive evidence of the good and regular standing, as a communicant, of any person, in all cases where, by the terms of this Charter, such standing is required as a qualification for voting.

Article Nineteenth. The clear yearly value or income of the real and personal estate held by the said Corporation shall not exceed at any time the sum of Ten thousand Dollars.

Article Twentieth. All property real and personal which shall be bequeathed, or devised, or conveyed to said Corporation, for the use of said Church, for religious worship or sepulture, or the maintenance of either, shall be taken held and inure, subject to the control and disposition of the lay members of said Church, or such constituted officers or representatives thereof as shall be composed of a majority of lay members, citizens of Pennsylvania, having a controlling power according to the rules, regulations, usages or corporate requirements thereof.

Article Twenty-first. Any amendment or amendments to this Charter shall be proposed at any annual or special meeting of the Corporation, and if agreed to by a majority of the qualified voters, then present in person, shall be entered upon the minutes of said meeting, with the number of voters given in favor and against the same, and the said amendment or amendments, shall again be laid before the next annual or special meeting of the said Corporation, and if the same shall then be adopted by three-fourths of the qualified voters, then present in person, such amendments or amendment shall be considered as finally agreed to, and it shall be the duty of the Trustees or any one of them to procure the ratification and sanction thereof by the proper authority. Provided always nevertheless that the foregoing provision is not to be construed, as authorizing any amendment or change in the second Article of this Charter, and it is hereby expressly agreed and declared that the second Article, or any part thereof shall not be subject to any alteration change or Amendment whatsoever.

ROBERT C. OGDEN,
WILLIAM L. COOKE
THEODORE H. LODER
JOHN K. FINDLAY
JAMES C. TAYLOR.

THE OLD TENTH CHURCH

In a sermon delivered November 7, 1858—
the twenty-fifth anniversary of his pastorate
over the Tenth Church—Dr. Henry A. Boardman thus spoke of the beginnings of that
important organization:

"The merit of proposing the erection of a
church on this spot [North-east corner of 12th
and Walnut streets] is due to the late Furman
Leaming. He associated with himself five
other gentlemen, namely, John Stille, of the
Second Church, George Ralston and James
Kerr, of the First Church, and William Brown
and Solomon Allen, of the Sixth Church.
Through the liberality and energy of these
six Christian men the work was accomplished.
The corner-stone was laid with appropriate
ceremonies by the late venerable Ashbel Green,
D.D., on the 8th of August, 1828.*

"On the 24th of May, following, the first
sermon was preached in the lecture-room by
Dr. C. C. Lansing. The building was com-

---

* In a manuscript found in the corner-stone when the church
was demolished in 1854, the date is given as *July 14th*, 1828, and
"*The Philadelphian*," of July 18, 1828, gives the same date.
H. P. F.

pleted on the 7th of December, 1829, and was opened for worship on the ensuing Sabbath, the 13th.''

Its pastors were : Thomas McAuley, D.D, LL.D., installed December 17th, 1829 ; Henry A. Boardman, D.D., ordained and installed November 8th, 1833 ; John DeWitt, D.D., installed October 12th, 1876 ; William Brenton Greene, Jr., D.D., the last pastor, installed May 14th, 1883. Dr. Greene's pastoral relation was, at his own request, dissolved by Presbytery December 5th, 1892, in order that he might accept the Stuart Professorship of the Relations of Philosophy and Science to the Christian Religion, in Princeton Theological Seminary. The church also had two associate pastors—Rev. Louis R. Fox, elected December 11th, 1871, and the Rev. J. Henry Sharpe, D.D., elected November 9th, 1874. Three of these pastors are still living : Drs. DeWitt and Greene, who are Professors in Princeton Theological Seminary ; and Dr. Sharpe, who is the pastor of the West Park Church, Philadelphia.

John S. Hart, LL.D., the distinguished author and educator, and the principal of the Philadelphia Boys' High School from 1842 to 1859, was, for a time, the superintendent of the Sunday-school. Richard H. Wallace was the last superintendent.

It is interesting to note that the first *night school* in this city, for the gratuitous instruction of young men, was established by members of the Tenth Church—an innovation which was afterwards adopted by the municipal authorities.

During Dr. Boardman's pastorate the church became very popular. The services were crowded, and it was often impossible to procure sittings. Special attention was given to visitors, medical students, and young ladies attending the seminaries. The church was also distinguished for its noble generosity. Not infrequently as much as $25,000 a year was contributed to benevolent objects. Between the years 1844 and 1873, 250 boxes filled with clothing, valued at $60,000, were sent out to missionaries.

The church was interested at various times in local mission enterprises, the most important of which was the one known as the Moyamensing Mission, and which developed into the Hollond Memorial Church. In 1856 a colony from the Tenth Church established the West Spruce Street Church.

In view of the encroachment of business houses, the consequent removal to a distance of many families of the congregation, and several other causes, the strength of the church gradually declined until finally at a congrega-

INTERIOR. OLD TENTH CHURCH

tional meeting held on the 3d of May, 1893, it was

"*Resolved*, That the work of this church be discontinued at this place, and that the church property at 12th and Walnut streets be sold at the earliest date that a good price can be obtained for it."

At a meeting of the congregation held on the 24th of May, of the same year, the following action was taken:

Resolved, That we offer the corporate title of the Tenth Presbyterian Church to the West Spruce Street Presbyterian Church.

Resolved, That when the property at Twelfth and Walnut streets be sold, $75,000 of the money be appropriated to the Hollond Presbyterian Church—$35,000 of the same to be applied to the payment of the church indebtedness, and $40,000 to be held as an endowment, protected by the language of the deed of the Tenth Presbyterian Church, which is as follows: "Provided always, that they shall adhere to and maintain the mode of faith and church discipline as set forth in the Confession of Faith of the Presbyterian Church in the United States of America."

Resolved, That the residue be given to the West Spruce Street Presbyterian Church as an endowment fund, protected by the language of the deed of the Tenth Presbyterian Church and to be held by trustees to be elected by the session and trustees of this church.

At its meeting on the 5th of June, 1893, the Presbytery recommended the Tenth Church to retain its corporate existence until the sale of the property; approved of the proposed ecclesiastical union between the Tenth Church and the West Spruce Street Church; and also approved of the arrangements adopted by the congregation for the disposal of the proceeds of the sale of the old church property.

On the 3d of June, 1895, Presbytery took the following final action:

Resolved, That the Tenth Presbyterian Church and the West Spruce Street Presbyterian Church be and the same are hereby united and merged into each other, and consolidated into one church to be known hereafter as the Tenth Presbyterian Church.

In the spring of 1894 the old church was sold for $150,000, of which amount Hollond, in accordance with the second of the above resolutions, received $75,000 and the West Spruce Street Church about $70,000.

The Sunday-school of the old Tenth held its sixty-fourth and last anniversary on Sunday afternoon, May 7, 1893. An interesting programme was prepared, which consisted of responsive reading and singing, and addresses by Mr. Richard H. Wallace, superintendent; Professor Robert Ellis Thompson, D.D., and Dr. Wm. M. Paden.

In introducing Dr. Paden, Mr. Wallace said: "The Tenth Church and Hollond have been linked together by the most intimate and closest of ties—that of mother and child. With pardonable pride we have watched and rejoiced over the marvellous progress Hollond has made in the past, and which we believe it is destined to make in the years to come; it is therefore with peculiar pleasure that we welcome Dr. Paden, who has done so much to make that progress possible.''

A touching incident occurred during the closing exercises. It was plainly evident that the older members felt the impressiveness of the hour; hallowed thoughts of other days were crowding thick and fast upon them; much that they loved and reverenced was in the clasp of the dead years; and the old church building, so dear to their hearts and about which clustered so many thronging and haunting associations, would soon be but a slowly fading memory. As if in sympathy with the solemn hour, the sun had gone behind a cloud, and a softened and subdued light came through the dim, time-stained windows, which seemed, like the weary eyes of an old man, to look down wonderingly and full of retrospective melancholy upon the assembled worshippers. But just as the congregation joined in the hymn, ''Jesus, Saviour, Pilot Me,'' with an earnestness which plainly indicated that it was sung as a heartfelt prayer for future help and guidance, a flood of sunlight broke through the cloud and fell like a benediction upon the flower-wreathed pulpit, the bright faces of the children, and the bowed heads of the old. Coming as it did with the lines—

"May I hear Thee say to me,
Fear not, I will pilot thee,"

it seemed prophetic of answered prayer and of continued blessings for the dear old church, for the boys and girls, and for those who were

"Only waiting till the angels
Open wide the mystic gates."

The old building was torn down in the summer of 1894 to make way for the erection of the Episcopal Diocesan House. When the corner-stone was removed in August of that year, the following interesting paper was found in a glass jar hermetically sealed:

"The corner-stone of the Tenth Presbyterian Church was laid July 14, 1828, in the city of Philadelphia, by Ashbel Green, a minister of the gospel of said city, John Quincy Adams being President of the United States, John Andrew Shultz, governor of the State of Pennsylvania, and Joseph Watson, mayor of Philadelphia.

"The enterprise of building this house for the public worship of Almighty God was conceived, undertaken, and the funds for the erection of the same were principally furnished by

the following gentlemen, who acted as a building committee, viz: John Stille, Furman Leaming, James Kerr, Solomon Allen, George Ralston, William Brown. In the erection of this
edifice the architect was William Strickland;
the carpenter and builder, James Leslie; the
bricklayers, A. & E. Robbins. When the stone
was laid the inhabitants of the United States
were enjoying perfect peace, and zealously engaged in promoting agricultural, mechanical,
and industrial improvements, associations, and
enterprises. Steamboat navigation was much
in use. Of our canals and railroads some were
completed and many more were planned and
commenced. For the promotion of good morals
and Christian piety infant Sunday-schools and
Bible classes had been instituted, the Bible and
tract societies formed; missions, both domestic
and foreign, commenced and successfully pros-
ecuted.

"The Presbyterian Church in the United
States, under the care of the General Assembly, consisted of 16 Synods, 90 Presbyteries,
1,285 ministers, 1,968 congregations, and
146,308 communicants. The house of which
this is the corner-stone, is ever to be considered as dedicated to the worship of the one
only living and true God, Father, Son and
Holy Ghost. In it no doctrine ought ever to
be taught, no worship ever attempted, not

consistent with a belief of the unity and personality of the Godhead, the natural and deep depravity of man, the atonement and intercession of the Lord Jesus Christ, the indispensable necessity of the renewing and sanctifying influences of the Holy Spirit in life, sincere obedience to all the commands of God, and a future state of endless rewards and punishments. And may many souls be won to God in this His temple on earth that shall be translated to the glorious worship and eternal bliss of 'the house not made with hands, eternal in the heavens.' "

THE PRESENT TENTH CHURCH

(Formerly the West Spruce Street Church)

BY REV. MARCUS A. BROWNSON, D. D.

The present Tenth Church is the result of a union of the Tenth Presbyterian Church and the West Spruce Street Presbyterian Church. This union was consummated as follows: By vote of the Tenth Church, May 24, 1893 ; by vote of the West Spruce Street Church, June 7, 1893; by vote of the Presbytery of Philadelphia, June 3, 1895 ; by action of the Court of Common Pleas, September 16, 1895.

The purpose of this chapter is to give a brief sketch of the West Spruce Street Church from its organization to the time of the consolidation with the Tenth Church; and of the united church since that date. Sketches heretofore published have been used freely in the preparation of this chapter.

On the 20th of January, 1852, a number of gentlemen connected with the Tenth Presbyterian Church met at the house of the pastor, Rev. Henry A. Boardman, D. D., to confer

upon the duty of establishing a new Presbyterian church in the city.

The Tenth Church, as stated in the preceding chapter, had been the result of a small
colonization from the First, Second and Sixth
churches. Originating in the foresight of only
six persons, it had become a large and prosperous congregation, with a communicant membership of more than 500 and a Sabbath-school
numbering nearly 700 teachers and scholars.
The feeling became strong that the church
ought to establish another church by sending
off a colony of members. Accordingly the
above-mentioned conference was held, and a
committee appointed to carry this purpose into
effect. The committee consisted of the follow-
ing-named gentlemen : James B. Ross, Singleton A. Mercer, Morris Patterson, James Murphy, Thomas Hoge and James Imbrie, Jr.
This committee, in due time, decided to locate
the church in what was then the southwest-
ern section of the city, and accordingly, in
June, 1852, a suitable lot was secured on the
southwest corner of Spruce and Seventeenth
streets.

On the 26th of April, 1855, the corner-stone
of a church edifice was laid by the Rev. Dr.
Boardman, assisted by clergymen of various
evangelical denominations. In due time the
present edifice was completed. The architect

was John McArthur, Jr., and the contractor John McArthur.

Before the completion of the church or chapel building, the organization of "the West Spruce Street Church " had been effected. Application having been made to the Presbytery of Philadelphia for the organization of the church, the purpose was accomplished by a committee of the Presbytery consisting of Rev. Drs. Boardman, Engles, and Rev. Mr. Shields, together with Messrs. Paul T. Jones and James Dixon, who, in the name of the Presbytery, constituted the new church of thirty-four members of the Tenth Presbyterian Church, who had requested the Presbytery so to do.   The meeting for organization was held in the lecture-room of the Tenth Church, April 3, 1856.   James Imbrie, Jr., John S. Hart and Morris Patterson were elected elders ; John McArthur, Jr., was elected a deacon ; and the Rev. William Pratt Breed, then of Steubenville, Ohio, was chosen, by vote of the congregation, as the pastor.   The charter of the congregation having provided that the pastor should be chosen by the persons subscribing to the application for the act of incorporation, a meeting of the said subscribers had been held on February 14, 1856, at which time it was unanimously resolved to call Mr. Breed to the pastorate of the church when it should be organized.

On the 29th of March, 1856, a charter was obtained, in which the following gentlemen were named as trustees: Moses Johnson, Morris Patterson, Singleton A. Mercer, John R. Vodges, James B. Ross, James Murphy, William Brown, William Goodrich, Theodore Cuyler, James Imbrie, Jr., Maurice A. Wurts, J. Engle Negus, John McArthur, Jr., John S. Hart and Anthony J. Olmstead.

The lecture-room of the West Spruce Street Church was opened for public worship on May 18, 1856; Rev. William P. Breed, the pastor-elect, preached the sermon. Rev. Dr. Boardman preached in the evening. One of the conditions upon which the thirty-four members of the Tenth Church consented to form the new organization was that the pastors of the two churches should exchange pulpit services once each Sabbath. This arrangement was continued for a number of years and until a protracted illness of Dr. Boardman brought it to a close.

The installation of Rev. William P. Breed as pastor of the church took place June 4, 1856, in the Tenth Church, the moderator of the Presbytery, the Rev. George W. Musgrave, D. D., presiding. Rev. Dr. Coleman gave the charge to the pastor ; the charge to the people was delivered by Dr. Boardman.

In the month of June of the same year, a Sabbath-school was organized, consisting of

exactly the same number of persons as originally composed the church, namely, thirty-four.
By appointment of the session, John S. Hart,
one of the elders, was made superintendent.
Professor Hart was an accomplished instructor,
being the principal of the Central High School
of Philadelphia. His character and work gave
a tone to the school which has continued ever
since.

The church edifice was dedicated to the worship of Almighty God on the first Sabbath of
January, 1857. The pastor preached, morning
and evening. At the afternoon service the
preacher was the Rev. John M. Krebs, D. D.,
of New York, of whose church at one time Mr.
Breed had been a member.

The church building is rectangular in form,
constructed of brick, with brown stone trimmings, and has the tallest spire of any church
in the city. A chapel and Sabbath-school
building are in the rear.

For more than thirty years the pastorate of
Dr. Breed continued, until, at his own request,
he became pastor emeritus, November 7, 1887.
His death occurred February 14, 1889. The
funeral service in the church was attended by
a large concourse of ministers and prominent
laymen of the city. The members of the congregation, to whose needs he had ministered
so long and so faithfully, were present in full

numbers to testify, by reverent silence and with tears, their devoted love to his character, life and labors in the Gospel.

Dr. Breed's ministry in the church was one of strong and wide influence and ever-increasing power. He was held in honor for his literary work, for his leadership in the courts of the Church, for his influential advocacy of matters of morals and of public interest appealing to his judgment and conscience ; but he was held in highest honor among his own people for his singularly pure character, his faithful preaching of the Gospel, and his tender, devoted pastoral work.

The West Spruce Street Church has been unusually fortunate in its eldership. Men of intellectual strength and of the highest moral character and spiritual excellence have held this office, and have guided the spiritual affairs of the church with the most efficient counsels and devoted labors, certain ones among them bestowing also most liberal gifts of money for the maintenance of the church and the extension of the Redeemer's kingdom beyond the boundaries of their particular congregation. The Patterson Memorial Presbyterian Church, in West Philadelphia, is the result of a gift of $30,000 by the will of Morris Patterson, Esq., placed in the hands of the trustees of the West .Spruce Street Church, to establish a church wherever they might think a Presbyterian church was required. The Church of the Evangel, at Eighteenth and Tasker streets, and the Presbyterian church at Fox Chase were established through the gifts of Gustavus S. Benson, Esq. Suitable mural memorials of these noble men of God are to be found in the Tenth Church—one on either side of the beautiful stone pulpit erected to the memory of Dr. Breed by his loving people.

After the death of Dr. Breed, a call was extended to the Rev. James D. Paxton, of Schenectady, N. Y., and, having accepted the same, he was installed as pastor, January 14, 1891.

During Mr. Paxton's pastorate the church was remodeled and very beautifully ornamented in the interior. The decorations are of the Byzantine order of the period from the eighth to the tenth century. The whole effect is pleasing and worshipful.

It was during Mr. Paxton's pastorate that the union with the old Tenth Church was effected. In 1896 Mr. Paxton resigned the pastoral charge of the church, to become the pastor of the American students in the Latin Quarter of Paris, where he remained for two years. Dr. Paxton is now pastor of the House of Hope Presbyterian Church, St. Paul, Minn.

The present officers of the church are :

PASTOR—Rev. Marcus A. Brownson, D. D.,

called from the pastorate of the First Presbyterian Church in Detroit, Mich., and installed March 30, 1897.

ELDERS—George Junkin, LL.D., (1861); John D. McCord (1870); Frank K. Hipple (1883); Edward Smith Kelley (1891); Wm. W. Moorhead, M. D., (1891); Isaac Shipman Sharp (1891); Richard H. Wallace (1893).

DEACONS—James Johnston (1890); Gustavus S. Benson, Jr., (1890); J. Howard Breed (1890).

TRUSTEES—George Junkin, president; Edward Smith Kelley, secretary; Frank K. Hipple, treasurer; John D. McCord, R. Dale Benson, Edward P. Borden, Henry C. Fox, Henry Maule, Isaac Shipman Sharp, D. F. Woods, M. D., W. Atlee Burpee, Strickland L. Kneass, Kenneth M. Blakiston.

The membership of the church numbers 641; and there are enrolled 320 scholars in the Sabbath-school, of which Mr. Frank K. Hipple is the superintendent.

The church has always been known as zealous for the support of the Boards of the Church at large. The benevolent contributions during the Church year of 1898–99 were as follows: Home Missions, $5758; Foreign Missions, $4429; Education, $464; Sabbath-school Work, $429; Church Erection, $283; Ministerial Relief, $1877; Freedmen, $288; Synodical Aid,

$263; Aid for Colleges, $339; General Assembly Expenses, $91; Bible Society, $110; Miscellaneous, $2641 ; total, $16,972.

It is thus apparent that the thirty-four members of the old Tenth Church builded better than they knew when they established the West Spruce Street Church, and it seemed most appropriate that when, by reason of depletion (through the inevitable changes of her own neighborhood) removal became necessary, the Tenth Church should seek union with the church which had come out from her thirty-seven years before, and that mother and child should again live and labor together in one happy spiritual family.

www.ingramcontent.com/pod-product-compliance
Lightning Source LLC
Chambersburg PA
CBHW030857270326
41929CB00008B/461